Books by Felipe Cofreros, Ph.D.

Children's Picture Books

The Hungry Frog
Danny the Deer
Blue Bird
Blue Bird Finds New Friends
Blue Bird and the Bees
Blue Bird and Black Bird
The Little Birds Help a Friend
The Boastful Rooster
Smart Ratty
Ollie and His Ball
Ollie Lost His Ball
Fix It Tipsie
Sam's Wish
Curious Sam
Sam and the Little Bird
Sam and the Hawk
Jackie's New Toy

Other Books

A Pre – school Math Workbook: Let's Start Building Our Math Skills Workbook (For Three Years Old and Up)

A Handbook of Basic Art, Part I (Painting Processes in the Playing With colors, Different Crayon Techniques)

A Handbook of Basic Art, Part II (Basic Drawing, Painting and making Crafts)

Let's Weave (An Ancient Hand Art of Interlacing Two Groups of Thread

Inside Japan: It's People and Culture

Effective Ways to Assess English Language Learners (For Intermediate and Advanced Levels)

A Handbook of Writing Activities for Intermediate and Advanced English Language, Learners

One Accord - An Inspirational Book of Bible Promises

A Handbook of Valuable Activities for Seniors

Refugee Resettlement in a Multi – Ethnic Society Part I

REFUGEE RESETTLEMENT IN A MULTI-ETHNIC SOCIETY PART 1

by Felipe Cofreros Ph.D.

Order this book online at www.trafford.com
or email orders@trafford.com

Most Trafford titles are also available at major online book retailers.

Senior Editor: Ronald Jay Blassingame Ph.D.
Associate Editor: Felipe Cofreros Ph.D.
Title Design: Charlene Rose Escolango Cofreros
Chaplain Romeo Tomas Salovino M.A. BCC
Cornelius Hiponia Cofreros

Print information available on the last page.

ISBN: 978-1-4907-9673-4 (sc)
ISBN: 978-1-4907-9674-1 (e)

Trafford rev. 11/12/2019

www.trafford.com
North America & international
toll-free: 1 888 232 4444 (USA & Canada)
fax: 812 355 4082

FOR CORNELIUS H. COFREROS AND CHARLENE ROSE E. COFREROS

CONTENTS

ILLUSTRATIONS

Maps

Exhibits

PREFACE

Upon arrival at the Philippine Refugee Processing Center to assume duties as an instructional teacher in the work orientation program with the International Catholic Migration Commission [ICMC], I discovered that the refugee center consists of 17,000 refugees at any given time made my presence a rarity. Being one of the instructional staff in a refugee processing center in Southeast Asian [SEA], I found myself confronted with the question: To what degree would my identity factor being an Asian who studied in a University with an American curriculum into my professional role. It seemed that sharing my perspective with others culturally different from myself would be a natural expression of my personality and multicultural experience and not at every moment "conscious" behavior. I had to also face the fact that this made me an enigma. I thought I had the necessary basic interpersonal skills to deal with some expected intercultural problems, however, shortly after my arrival I was forced to concede that given that I was interfacing at least four [4] different cultures [Vietnamese, Cambodian, Laotian and Hmong] my skills were not sufficient. I am not sure to what degree this had an initial impact on how I approached and handled my work. I can say that my acting to improve my intercultural communication skills by becoming familiar with the language and cultures I needed to know, was helpful as well as being a humbling experience. In this regard, this placed me on even footing with many others in the refugee camp who were "struggling" to understand and be understood in a new culture. Several people played a significant role during my experience at the Philippine Refugee Processing Center and inspired me to undertake this study. They viewed my presence at the refugee camp as valuable for the refugees and the international staff and also had the insight to know that I had a strong need to share my observations and many questions. They were knowledgeable of the American perspective and how it could make a "positive" contribution to the SEA refugee education and resettlement effort. Ronald Jay Blassingame Ph.D. was a valued mentor that believed in my difficulty to undertake this research endeavor and made his time available to me as my technical advisor. As my work orientation supervisor, immediately began to speak to my intermitted doubts about having the will to complete the research for this project, particularly when I was unsuccessful in unearthing vital information in order to move ahead. On several occasions and with great inconvenience to himself, he got the data I needed. Without his assistance, it would not have been possible to bring this project to closure. His keen perception and comprehensive understanding of the issue involved in this study made me to pursue this study. Since he saw it as my most important project, I am indebted to him for taking the time to get to know my thoughts so well that he came to my fears. Thank you for helping me do what I had to do. I am grateful for his friendship and support.

A profound debt of gratitude is owed to Sharon Christine Snyder Ph.D. a professor and director of the English Department English as a Second Language [ESL] Program at Kean University in Union, New Jersey, USA for personally looking over my preliminary research notes and arranging for me to confer with her colleagues whose suggestions and insights valuable to this project.

The Honorable Attorney Lemuel Carlos helped me to define and better understand some of the legal dimensions this study would touch on, provided I were posing the right questions. I will remember always that once I was in his company he gave me the sense that he had all the time in the world to give to me.

Heartfelt thanks is owed to the American Studies Association of the Philippines [ASAP] for the never ending support it provided and for its recognition of this project in the area of Philippine-American studies. ASAP served as one of the central forces behind the founding [1986] of the Bata-an Chapter of ASAP where I had the honor to serve as one of its members.

I thank Yolanda Delariarte DeStefano Ed.D., and Janet Villagomez Ph.D. who supported my involvement an "experimental" academic program: Experimental Program in Independence Study [EPIS], - this is how it all began for me - by acting as my mentors. They have left an indelible imprint on my life; namely, for having shared with me ideas and visions for what my life could be. Were it not for them, I might not found myself on fire and believing a sense of purpose, passion, and patience could take me in life most anywhere I wanted to go. I am grateful to God for bringing these extraordinary people into my life at a time when I was struggling to define myself and develop.

Last, but not least, I thank Hope Villanueva Blassingame and Elma Escolango Cofreros for the editorial work they did on the drafts this project went through. And to my son Cornelius H. Cofreros and his wife Caroline Cuarenta Cofreros and my daughter Charlene Rose E. Cofreros for being my cheering squad from day one.

Felipe Cofreros, Ph.D.

ACKNOWLEDGMENTS

"Refugee Resettlement In a Multi-Ethnic Society" records the essence of my being an English a Second Language (ESL) teacher for a decade in the International Catholic Migration Commission (ICMC), Philippine Refugee Processing Center (PRPC), Sabang, Morong, Bataan, Philippines.

I dedicate this book to my English as a Second Language (ESL) co-teachers and Supervisors in the International Catholic Migration Commission (ICMC), Philippine Refugee Processing Center (PRPC) in Sabang, Morong, Bataan, Philippines: Andy Reyes Ed.D.; Oliver Colmenar; John Duffy; Yolanda Delariarte De Stefano Ed.D.; Nestor Tebio M.A; Lazaro Omalin; Marilyn Omalin; May San Juan Soriano, Ronald Jay BLassingame, Ph.D.; Hope Villanueva Blassingame; Mel Thaib Globio; Beda Vergara, Elizabeth Bernaldez Bacarro; Perla Santos; Carmen Dantes; Thomas Rogers; Matsy Tumacdang Alvanto; No Cabading Lim; Bonifacio Jose; Delilah Borja; Greg Taag; Laurie Kuntz; Jessie Ponce; Leonila Portugal; Ed Espiritu; Marlon Patalagsa; Victoria Pardo Long; Candido Magnaye; Necessita Garchitorena; Emmanuel Jesus Villanueva; Olaf Bautista; Gorgonia Ledesma Pe; Rex Pe; Rey Medenilla; Jess Diaz Israel; Jimmy Sevalla; James Tuttle; Lydia Ferrer, Rosemarie Parreno; Eden Mag-aro Mclean, John Borja; Imelda Orda Schwartz; Ben Ramos; Celedonio Cofreros Campos; Edith Cervantes Bowen; Rose Velez; Evelyn Gustilo Costa, Natividad Yusay; Rodolfo Macasinag; Cynthia De Velez; Demetrio Alburo; Mary Ann Obfenda; Helen Jarandillo; Leonor Antoja Verano; William Joseph Guingona; Edna Diolata; Amalda Ada; Milady Villaflor – Dennison; Edith Silva Smith; Farah Priela; Teresita Magbanua – Shafer; Victoria Rafael Gilbertson; John Shafer; Juliana Merafuentes; Anniefe Liveta Rodriguez; Jovy De La Paz; Robert Salter; Faina Salter; Guada Marquez; Lorna Blancaflor;

Jesusa Juen Hafford; Estella Alesna Ohlrogge; Edda Octaviano; Adlai Castigador, Ph.D; Christina Arcilla; Ligaya Escobar Padua; Tessie Provido Padilla; Gener Zamora; Fabie Dionela; Be Jensen; Wilma Limbag; Marlon Ibao; Lilia Banez Tacorda; Evangeline Michell; Benji Romero; Joni Vivar; Maluz Lupisan Aponte; Nancy Bautista-Saxton; Mila Santos; Joy Pader; Victor Edrosolan; Linda Day; Rosalie Casis Woolley; Evelyn Diaz; Albert Lupisan, Ph.D.; Evelyn Labitag; Corazon De Villa; Lourdes Marquez; Babes Katima; Chona Bollos; Irene Gaston, M.A.; Lucy Evangelista; Ann Thu; Merle Rabelas; Nimfa Zafe; Al Pena; Al Medina; Lolita Gamboa; Myrna Divinagracia; Nimfa Litonjua; Sylvia Ivy Velvet; Norma Padua; Carmen Sorra-Emerenciana; Gloria Leal; Gloria Imperial; Edwin Fajardo; Annie Rivera; Ceres Fern Demegilio; Noy Demegilio; Lynette Barit-Demegilio; Chi Reimer; Linette Pascual Paras; Nick Gonzaga; Mel Tagudar-Corkum; Alejandro Racelis; Susan Sepulchre Turner; Rafael Sepulchre; Susan Togle Kostoleski; Ernie Baron Puguon; Melba Pedrosa; Gat Alaliit; Angie Parentila; Lumen Pascual; Martin Legaspi Bancaya; Francisca Pillazar; Rolf Klemm; Me-An Sabares Klemm; Nora Nidea-Gallano; Gabriela Starker-Saxe, M.A.; Jo Otica-Sillorequez; Charlie Antonio; Tristan Bautista; Angelina Bagares; Merlotte Mountecillo; Henry Viola; Barry Wicksman; Francisco Balasabas; Corazon Balasabas; Leda Denamarquez; Bani Ambion; Joel Galicano; Nona Bollos; Thelma Rodriguez; Reuben Tinio; DaleBuscher; Chito Mandia; Elizabeth Sison Tyrell; Josephne Hufana; Margaret Ponti; Suchat Katima; Gary McLean; Ernie Gelvoria; Fernando De Sagun; Rodil Tolentino; Dave Tolson; Chito Atienza; Sam Falsis; Sam Salter; Joey Jose; Joseph Taraba; Susan Guinto; Doris Ammon; Ramon Lim; Ramona Lamo; Siena Bustos; Marissa Castro – Pasive; Norlita Orbien; Ruel Bacarro; Violeta Piduan; Natividad Pagud Guarco; Edith Montanez; Eva Servando; Adorma Orlain; Relly Perez Aldon; Corazon Pasaraba Zinampan; Mary Ann Mizal Hidalgo; Diane Bruckner; Marjorie Sutton; Jack Bumgardner; Delia Batalao; Dave Perrin; Margot Evidente Perrin; Lydia Bumgardner; Rob Dira; Eddie Pal; Erlinda Garganilla; Danilo Baylen; Linor Lineses; Maricel Janda; Tess Cardel Chand; Blandina Guttierez Rodriguez; Butch Nayona; Grace Tupaz Gelvoria; Grace Valenzuela; Grace Miras Heacock; Fred Heacock; and Lourdes Stevens.

I am Grateful to the following professional educators for their review part of the text. Dr. Ronald Jay Blassingame, Ph.D; Hope

Villanueva Blassingame; Yolanda Delariarte De Estefano, Ed.D.; Andy Reyes, Ed.D; and Chaplain Romeo Tomas Salovino, BCC.

Finally, I am grateful to Elma Escolango Cofreros for her enthusiasm, ideas, graciousness, guidance and encouragement during this project along with indispensable advice, comments, evaluation and review, and Charlene Rose Escolango Cofreros, who painstakingly edited the manuscript's early drafts, enhancing content, style and comprehensibility for our readers.

Felipe Cofreros, Ph.D.

FOREWORD

The focus of this descriptive analysis is on the organizational framework of the largest Cultural Orientation [CO] project in the world implemented by the International Catholic Migration Commission [ICMC], which was contracted by the United States Department of State, Bureau for Refugee Programs, to conduct refugee resettlement education in Bata-an, the Republic of the Philippines for Indo-Chinese refugees bound for resettlement in the United States of America. From 1980 to 1990, ICMC/Philippines provided Cultural Orientation to a quarter of a million Indo-Chinese refugees. This inquiry establishes and clarifies what were some of the assumptions which contributed to the conceptualization of CO program instruction for adult Southeast Asian refugees intended to help the refugee achieve positive adjustment to life in the United States of America. The salient questions addressed in this research are: [1] What is overseas refugee education? [2] How is it constructed and conceptualized? [3] How is it practiced and implemented? and [4] Can the Philippines Refugee Processing Center serve as model for preparing refugees to live in a Western multi-ethnic society? Postulated in the analysis are the strengths and weaknesses of the following elements staff training and development, educational theory, and refugee resettlement.

Hypothesis testing of selected program elements and replication design of the locus of the program leading to conceptualization of refugee education include: selected case studies, surveys [statistical and quantitative], policy review and analysis, personal interviews and legal opinions.

The findings of this field-based research support the original hypothesis that certain operational concepts of American Cultural Orientation [CO] were "dysfunctional" and "incompatible" with the goals of preparing Southeast Asian refugees for successful adjustment to living in the United States of America. Moreover, the findings will be useful to U.S. Government officials, educators, researchers and refugee resettlement professionals who will consider the value of this study from the perspective of a naturalized American citizen whose country of origin is the Republic of the Philippines.

Felipe Cofreros, Ph.D.

ABOUT THE AUTHOR

Felipe Cofreros, Ph.D.

Felipe Cofreros spent twenty five years of aggregate experience in teaching literacy, adult education, pre-school, elementary, high school, college and the administration of instructional English as a Second language [ESL] services among Indo-Chinese refugees [Vietnamese, Lao, Khmer and Hmong] in the International Catholic Migration Commission [ICMC], Philippine Refugee Processing Center [PRPC] in Sabang, Morong, Bata-an, Philippines for a decade. Felipe also taught English as a Second Language [ESL] in different countries in Asia and North America: Saint Mary College in Nagoya City, Japan for two years; Regent College and Pannasastra University of Cambodia in Samdech Pann, Phnom Penh, Kingdom of Cambodia for two years; The United Nations [UN] Language Center in Dili City and Manufahi district in East Timor for two years; Zoni Language Centers in Manhattan and Queens, New York City, New York, United States of America [USA] for seven years and Effective Tutoring Systems in Las Vegas, Nevada, United States of America for three years.

Felipe's vast experience as a curriculum developer in Arts and Crafts program in the International Catholic Migration Commission [ICMC], Preparation for the American Secondary School [PASS] Program in the Philippine Refugee Processing Center in Sabang, Morong, Bata-an, Philippines; Saint Mary College in Nagoya City, Japan; University of Saint La Salle in Bacolod City, Philippines; La Consolacion College in Bacolod City, Philippines and Assumption Convent School in Iloilo City, Philippines greatly contributed to the creation of the following books that he wrote: A Handbook of Basic Art, Part 1 [Painting Processes in Playing with Colors, Different Crayon Techniques]; A Handbook of Basic Art, Part II [Basic Drawing, Painting and Making Crafts] and Let's Weave [An Ancient Hand Art of Interlacing Two Groups of Threads]. He has also written more than a dozen of Children's Picture Books with illustrations and comprehension questions: A Pre-school Math Workbook "Let's Build Our Math Skills Workbook" For children ages three years old and up; Inside Japan: Its People and Culture and Effective Ways To Assess English Language Learners [For Intermediate and Advanced Levels].

Felipe graduated as scholar or its equivalent to cum laude from the University of San Agustin in Iloilo City, Philippines with a Bachelor of Science in Elementary Education with specialization in Social Studies and Art Education. He got his Latin, Spanish and Theology courses at the Seminary of San Agustin in Intramuros, Manila, Philippines and a Master of Arts credits in Language and Literature Program, Teaching English as a Second Language [ESL] in De La Salle University in Manila, Philippines.

He got his Master's Degree in TESOL and Doctor of Philosophy in Sociology from an on-line university in the U.S.A.

Felipe obtained quite a number of certificates in different disciplines such as: TESOL Teaching Certificate Course, Lingua Edge, LCC, TESOL Teacher Training Systems at West Olympic Blvd., Beverly Hills, California, USA; Managing People for Maximum Performance in John F. Kennedy School of Management, Harvard University in Cambridge, Massachusetts, USA; The Roots of Learning: Society for Effective Affective Learning in Brighton, England, United Kingdom; Basic Japanese Language and Japanese Sumie Art in Saint Mary College, Nagoya City, Japan and the New Role of Art in Education in the University of the Philippines in Iloilo City, Philippines.

By M. Pulido
Source: Amerasia Journal, 1989

PART ONE

A Matter Of Socio-Cultural And Political Circumstances: Two Enduring Views Complete

CHAPTER I

Review of the Literature

The present literature on Southeast Asian (SEA) refugee resettlement education, its conceptual issues and assumptions, has significantly defined itself in terms of pedagogical and organizational theory and practice in a relatively short span of time from 1980 to 1995 (Morgan, 1995). It has generally moved with greater clarity in being able to identify its core element which is to impart knowledge to these particular refugees who have low education and job skill level about a social process of acquiring a positive adjustment in a western multi-ethnic society as America (IRAC, 1987; Morgan, 1985 (b)).

Reference to the mental health status of the SEA refugees in their first eighteen months in the U.S. indicates that the adjustment process severely tests their newly learned coping skills (Baker, et al, 1983; Lin and Minoru, 1983; Refugee Service Center, 1986; Rumbaut, 1985). Because of this, educators and practitioners of cross-cultural training have expressed their notions about what proper steps of preparation, important resettlement issues and practical concepts need to be taught. They recognize the value of experience being the best teacher, and that it is not possible to teach the refugee everything he needs to know or to assume solutions to individual needs in preparing for the unknown.

Any serious inquirer who endeavors to arrive at a coherent and basic understanding of the refugee experience from his processing in SEA to his resettlement in America, will invariably have to face a number of critical issues having to do with "intercultural education for multicultural societies" (Albert and Triandis, 1985; Cory, 1986; Hofsted; 1986; McCaffery, 1986; Stein, 1981; Tollefson, 1986). Whatever construct he chooses, he will take into account the uniqueness of the refugee education which embodies a host of definitions and assumptions (Friere, 1968; Hughes-Wiener, 1986; Hunter, 1982; RMC, 1984; Starr and Roberts, 1981).

The International Catholic Migration Commission (ICMC) was one of the agencies, and the largest in size, contracted by the U.S. Department of State, to conduct overseas (Southeast Asia) refugee education. It constructed the theoretical, instructional, and practical concepts of cultural orientation for instructional implementation from 1980 to 1995 (Ranard and Pfleger, 1995). The program implemented targeted elements in refugee resettlement education: staff training and development, educational theory, and refugee resettlement. Both means of implementing the component itself. Ideally, the desired objective and training system used was to leave the refugee at the stage where he should have gained self-confidence to be able to positively engage or assimilate in a multi-ethnic western milieu (Cory, 1986; Forbes, 1985).

As of 1985, the thrust of cultural orientation in SEA refugee processing centers (RPC) placed the refugee adult learner along the lines of experiential learning; whereby, he could gain additional guidance and practice in being able to conceptualize social problems of a western import and actively seek for the appropriate solutions. This learning approach was not traditional in that the learner was not made to strive to become more rational, critical, detached and more adept at manipulation of words, symbols and abstraction, or acquiring an intellectual understanding of cultural diversity. Instead, he was taught how to make decisions with less than complete information, to find ways to communicate in an unfamiliar system, so as to cope with the demands of a cross-cultural situation (Hughes-Wierner, 1986). The basic components of the refugee educational theory of refugee education became a basis of struggle among educators in their desire to create a balanced instructional training system through which educational content was delivered (Blassingame, 1984; Blume, 1987; Gochenour and Janeway, 1977; Hughes-Wierner, 1986; Tollefson, 1986; Walsh, 1985). Subsequently, there was a move to redesign the focus of overseas cultural orientation to fashion it to be a better instructional tool for positive refugee resettlement: one rationale was to resolve the perceived American public opinion that refugees had become dependent on the welfare system (Brimelow, 1995; Harmon, 1995; Morgan, 1995). The ideal indicator of successful refugee resettlement could be correlated to the number of those that got off of welfare after their first eighteen months in the U.S. The Effects of Pre-entry Training on the Resettlement of Indochinese: Final Report (RMC, 1984) suggests that the resettled refugee perceived no hurry whatever to cut short his connection with the welfare system, due to the belief that they were "entitled" to it (Blass, 1986).

Suffice to say, the SEA overseas refugee program were caught in a precarious position in that public opinion could determine how they would move and in what direction (Harmon, 1995; Morgan, 1995). The refugee welfare issue (Blass, 1986; Refugee Reports, 1988 (d); Wiemer, 1991) had, to a noticeable extent, a negative unintended outcome in that overseas resettlement orientation "formally" introduced refugees to the welfare system with the intent to educate them about it, only to have to deal with the fact that many of them, once resettled in America, seemed to develop a dependency to it (McCafferty, 1986). Subsequently, with the overseas PRC dimension, whether in actual fact, cultural orientation on its own merits, could be realistically expected to convey to the refugee the social and socio-political issues involved in welfare, as well as the negative social pathology it had been known to foster (Clark, 1965; Wilson, 1987), remained to be seen. This issue alone had made the overseas refugee cultural orientation stand apart; hence, the concept had no realistic or comparable base from which to make such a projection.

The ICMC instructional program components tasked with cultural orientation: Preparation for American School System (PASS), Work Orientation (WO), and Cultural Orientation (CO), were likewise described as wrought with serious conceptual issues of: (1) program focus (McCafferty, 1986; Redding, 1985) (2) staff development (Albert, 1985; Blassingame, 1984; Blume, 1987; Maciel, 1985; Wederspahn, 1985; Wyly, 1986) and (3) educational theory (Tollefson, 1986; 1989 (b)). The cultural orientation components had as its locus the issue of postulating the "required" knowledge the refugees needed in order to be able to make the initial positive cultural adjustment to American life. In the beginning stages of the cultural orientation program, it was assumed that the implied generic definition of "orientation" (Bennett, 1986) would be sufficient to adequately prepare the refugee for resettlement by simply providing them information centered around the "who, what, where" and the "do's and don't's" of resettlement. Since there was no "process" element tied to this approach, the orientation did not have a clear instructional "behavioral" objective. It was difficult for the instructional staff to gain any clear sense of how the refugee might fare in the stateside resettlement process because the orientation was not intended to alter in any noticeable way the behavior of the refugee while in the learning environment of the RPC. On-going Department of State and other organization newsletter U.S. refugee resettlement publications: Information Update (RSC/CAL, 1986-87); The Bridge (IRAC, 1987); The Front Page (RSC/CAL, 1987) gave special attention to refugee adjustment to life in the U.S., indicating that more needed to be done in this area of preparing refugees for not only learning about America, but how to also deal with the uniqueness of problems stemming from a western multi-ethnic society.

The initial assumption that cultural information about the U.S. in itself was sufficient to contribute to positive adjustment, proved to be short-sight and rather limited (Redding, 1985). Redding in his capacity as one of the senior program administrators at ICMC/Philippines in 1985, faced this issue by setting cultural orientation program component in a "New Direction." The merits of incorporating new theoretical constructs and moving in another direction was necessary if the needs of the refugee were to be met. Bennett (1986), Gochenour and Janeway (1977); Redding (1985) pointed out the notion that in order to build a cultural orientation program, the ability to select a priority of subject matter content must balance with process elements that would provide the needed experiential learning to take place. This was also the beginning point of re-examining the new role of the instructional staff, namely, the teachers, would have to play.

While Redding had put in place the new theoretical foundation of cultural orientation, the following staff; Blassingame (1984); Maciel (1985); Wederspahn (1985) and Wyly (1986) tackled the issue of staff development as a spin-off of the cultural orientation redirection. They wrestled with conceptual issues related to the ICMC Training System (1988 (c)) charged with enabling instructional staff to know how to apply the learning theory in the classroom to their students. Without the benefit of understanding and clarity of purpose on the part of instructional staff, the CO program's "New Directions" could not be expected to go far.

The evolution of educational theory with particular reference to refugees, had brought with it unavoidably a good deal of chaos as part of an evolutionary process. A considerable amount of the confusion emanated from an educational theory that had more to do with staff "assumptions" about learning as well as what a SEA refugee needed to know to be able to make a positive adjustment to life in America (Morgan, 1995). Another significant observation was that for all the effort expended by the instructional staff, in the SEA setting of the refugee camp, western educational theories tended to break down because the practical utility of a given educational theory was difficult to define or demonstrate out of context to the given setting and culture. In this regard, the RPC presented a formidable challenge. Paulo Friere's educational treatise, though ideally suited for aiding the objectives of the resettlement process, had only limited success within the Philippine Refugee Processing Center (PRPC) milieu. The Friere model of "problem-posing" regarded as "revolutionary" in some quarters for raising the socio-political consciousness of the learner in the learning process, made learning anything but a passive experience. This fact, that the learning process and experience evolved out of a dynamic social force to empower the learner in a way that he had not quite known before, was bound by the limits of what could and could not be easily promoted in a refugee camp environment if the application was for stateside resettlement.

Madeline Hunter's (1982) theory of Mastery Teaching was the first instructional model used by ICMC/Philippines. It was adopted and modified for program-wide use in 1983. This model compared to the rest was thought by the management solid enough to contribute to the ICMC Guide for Instruction

(1985 (d)), which described how "quality" instruction was attained in the organization. It brought uniformity or standardization to instruction because prior to that, the teachers relied on their own individual resources and creativity. It embodied the "traditional" teacher-learner clear-cut roles and took a fundamental approach. It was reworked and expanded to address the unique needs of refugee adult learners and instructional staff. This was necessary, owing to the fact that although many staff could vouch for the fact that it was "tried and true," it was also believed that in the case of the refugee adult learner, it was seen as too simplistic. Nor would it lend itself readily for an adult to learn and become comfortable with being an "active" learner in a student-centered learning environment.

James Tollefson (1986; 1989 (a)) was one of the few educators in his tenure with ICMC who strived to bring some measure of clarity and insights to vexing problems having to do with assumptions about what educators believed students needed to learn (Harmon, 1995; Morgan 1995; Ranard and Pfleger, 1995). This was going to the heart of the matter because what instructional staff thought or believed ultimately became translated into "functional competencies" in the respective classrooms. No one at ICMC would deny the fact that problems in this area did exist and yet somehow the dominant thinking at that time, was that, to deal with it was to be overstepping one's bounds; that this was better left to the Department of State and/or Center for Applied Linguistics. Because this kind of thinking was prevalent, not many instructional staff was prepared or willing to discuss it in a serious and open manner.

There was one occasion when the writer met with an ICMC official sent to the PRPC by the ICMC/Washington, D.C. sub-office. Before getting down to the purpose for the meeting, his latest "news" out of Washington was about the Tollefson article: "Functional Competencies in the U.S. Refugee Program: Theoretical and Practical Problems" (1986) which had appeared in TESOL Quarterly. He explained that the day the article had reached the Center for Applied Linguistics (CAL), Washington, D.C. office, immediately everyone there refused to believe that anyone could write a "negative" article about overseas refugee education and have it published. According to him, some CAL staff went as far as saying that they would never again read another TESOL Quarterly. I could not help but form the impression that the frenzied sentiment was that, it was not possible for any pedagogical problems at ICMC/Philippines to exist, and anyone who said differently, "publically" deserved to be excommunicated. One month after hearing from many people of the uproar in Washington over the Tollefson article, TESOL held its annual convention in Miami, Florida. As customary, ICMC sent delegates to attend, to conduct workshops and present papers. The Program Officer from the Work Orientation program attended and on her return to ICMC/Philippines, gave a report to the staff. Of special note in her (verbal) report was the workshop led by Prof. James W. Tollefson of the University of Washington, which she and staff from CAL Washington, D.C. and Manila attended, where someone asked the question of Prof. Tollefson's concerns enumerated in his article (Tollefson, 1986) and if the problems were still unresolved. Before he could respond, the ICMC Work Orientation program officer took the liberty to inform all present that when Prof. Tollefson was with ICMC, the comments which he had made relative to the Pre-employment Training Program (PET), no longer applied because PET had since changed its name to Work Orientation (WO). The program officer's reasoning apparently was that the problem under PET should not be associated with the WO.

The writer found this report wanting, hard pressed upon hearing it, to be able to see in what way it was meant to advance what was a reasonable question. Subsequently, all he was able to gather from this statement was that a new name had the power to give a new lease on life. In the business world, this practice generally goes by the name of "bankruptcy." It would seem that Tollefson was on to something and refugee educators had real cause for concern (Blume, 1987).

The overreaction and negative criticism of some educators for Tollefson and others who had expressed their concerns and insights with the intention of helping build up the ICMC/Philippines program (Blassingame, 1984; 1987; Blume, 1987; Harrison, 1987 (a); Mitchell, 1987) only missed the points which were being raised, such as the pedagogical framework on the adult learner's needs and the existing training needs of the instructional staff (ICMC, 1986 (c); White, 1988).

Where "social democracy" was absent in the PRPC setting, even the educational theory and practice of Friere was only marginally successful. If educators themselves showed intolerance for exchange of ideas, how could students be demonstrated how to make their own way in a democratic society. The problem lay in teaching about an abstract concept as living in a free society with all its laws and belief systems entirely different from the known or familiar setting as the Philippines. The democracy in the Philippines should not be confused with the democracy of the West (Karnow, 1989, Proser, 1981). It is precisely the notion of "similarities" between American and Filipino cultures which tended to obscure perception of differences. For Filipino teachers to assume that they knew American culture and society when many of them had not been to the U.S. or even abroad, posed a complex problem affecting refugees and their future life in America.

For ICMC to assume that Filipino teachers could be provided the necessary and basic skills to do the job of cultural orientation (Maciel,

1985; White, 1988) was to task them not only with information dissemination but of processing it, involving problem-solving, decision-making, attitudes and values clarification, and the like (Hughes-Wiener, 1986). The learning transfer to the refugee, often intercepted by the teacher's own interpretation (Denton and Villena-Denton, 1986) resulted in unrealistic prejudicial stereotyping, hence, non-beneficial to the refugee student.

Meanwhile, educational theory and pedagogical development and implementation in ICMC continued to evolve in a precarious process, the organization received praises and accolades from the U.S. Department of State (Chau, 1988; Morgan, 1985; RMC, 1984) for its educational success in educating SEA refugees which for many serious educators was an indication of fundamentally sound curriculum and methodology. Inside and outside of ICMC they continued to assess the program with tests to correlate refugee educational attainment in overseas refugee programs at RPC's with successful resettlement in the U.S. It would be difficult to argue with those in powerful positions who needed to praise ICMC/Philippines for its educational achievement without regard for its flaws.

Relevant to the issue of using the PRPC as a model of a multi-ethnic society was the new voice of the few American minority-of-color in the community of international staff in the PRPC for a need to re-examine and reconsider the past, present and future conceptualization of a functional refugee multi-cultural education (Blassingame, 1987 (c); Harrison, 1987 (a); InterAction, 1991). The basis of which was the notion that existing issues and assumptions were formed from the perspective of the American dominant cultural group which was white (Hall, 1981; Kochman, 1981). An example of this was the common assumption (Brimelow, 1995; Fujiyoshi, 1989) that the only true Americans were the whites and their point of view prevailed and dominated in the general American culture. The refugees however, upon resettlement in America would find themselves merging into an environment with other minority-of-color groups and being classed as the same (Carter, 1990; Gross, 1991; Ronk, 1991; Wilson, 1987). This was one realization they had to also prepare for. The lack of minorities was not only reflected in the overseas refugee orientation instructional programming, but in the management and overall organizational system (White, 1988). This issue became a "controversial" struggle that was part of the experience of the research for this study.

The Problem

This study is a descriptive analysis of the American cultural orientation program conducted by the International Catholic Migration Commission for Southeast Asian refugees. The scope includes the curriculum, the implementation by the staff and the organization itself, its policies and pedagogical "assumptions" as a U.S. government sponsored project affected by the unpredictability of international events and American domestic and foreign policy.

The main concern of this study is the issue of how Southeast Asian refugees, Vietnamese, Cambodian and Laotians were taught American culture and society for the purpose of achieving psychological readiness and positive resettlement in the United States.

The International Catholic Migration Commission, a Geneva based agency, was contracted by the U.S. Department of State, Bureau for Refugee Programs to conduct the world's largest English-as-a-Second Language and Cultural Orientation American resettlement education program in Bataan, at the Philippine Refugee Processing Center. It opened in 1980 and closed in 1995, having served approximately half a million Southeast Asian refugees.

Its cultural orientation program objective was to prepare refugees for positive adaptation and resettlement in the U.S. by teaching them American customs and values; such as: self-reliance and freedom to enjoy life in a pluralistic multiethnic society. For refugee education to be functional, the policies and pedagogical assumptions of the program are analyzed. These were three (3) basic features of the program that challenged the achievement of its objectives:

1. The teaching staff was composed of almost all Filipino; many of whom were fresh college graduates, never traveled abroad

nor lived in the United States to be able to conceptualize American culture and society;

2. The curriculum was taught primarily by means of realia and pictures, no hands-on active participation or exposure to a more modern setting reflective of America; and
3. The lack of American minority-of-color representation in the workplace (ICMC/Philippines) and setting (Philippine Refugee Processing Center) for refugees to identify with as a minority group.

Significance of the Study

The significance of this study is two-fold. First is the "choice" of the subject matter: an analysis of the cultural orientation project of the International Catholic Migration Commission / Philippines and U.S. Department of State's Overseas Refugee Program. This project was "unique" in that for the first time, the American government chose to address on a large scale the refugee problem in Southeast Asia. From 1980 to 1995, approximately one million Vietnamese, Laotian, and Cambodian refugees studied in the camps in Hongkong, Thailand, Indonesia and the Philippines. It introduced the cultural orientation (CO) program component in its overseas refugee resettlement education program which formerly was solely English-as-a-Second Language based.

What previous knowledge and experience it had about refugee education projects based in Europe and Africa for Eastern Europeans and African migrants and refugees bound for resettlement in the U.S., was insufficient, making this new component an "experiment" in refugee education (Ranard and Pfleger, 1995). That it should address the need for pre-entry skills training for resettlement in U.S. of one million non-white refugees became the concern of the author who is an American minority-of-color, who became involved in refugee resettlement education from 1984 to 1991.

Secondly, the significance of this study is that the cultural orientation component of the U.S. overseas refugee resettlement program is analyzed "first-hand" from a minority-of-color perspective. The first reason is that the refugee themselves are classed as minorities in America, or that a majority of them start or live with other minority groups in the same neighborhoods or have close contact with them. The second reason is that the pedagogical assumptions of cultural orientation reflected the traditional dominant perspective of the white majority of the American population. An example of this common notion perpetuated was that the only real Americans were the whites, or assumed to be whites; while the rest were referred to as Blacks, Hispanics, Japanese, Chinese, Indians, etc., stereo-typing was common, for example: Blacks were to be feared by the refugees in America. Thirdly, relevant social issues on refugee resettlement in the U.S. as welfare dependency, racial tensions, the law and crime were not intensively processed in the overseas refugee education program.

Delimitations

The parameters of this investigation revolve around the conceptualization of what was the largest cultural orientation project component in the world. The other project components of the International Catholic Migration Commission / Philippines at the Philippine Refugee Processing Center: English-as-a-Second Language (ESL), Preparation for American School System (PASS) and Assistant Teacher Para-professional Training Program (ATPTP) are not within the domain of this study. Although PASS was classified as a cultural orientation program component and should fall within the preview of this study, but does not because the targeted student/learner group of this study is categorized as "adult" learners between the ages of 17 to 55 years. PASS learners were of a younger age group. ATPTP which handled refugee assistant teachers and language translators/ interpreters that provided the necessary instructional support i.e., language translation to instructional departments is not given a major focus in this study for the reason that it did not fall under the ICMC training system and was considered "advanced" adult learners and had resettlement concerns slightly different from those of the target group.

The setting for this inquiry is the Philippine Refugee Processing Center (PRPC) which has as its furthest geographical parameter, Southeast Asia (SEA), on one hand, and the United States, on the other. These two boundaries are the total universe from which the investigation may be placed in geographical, political, pedagogical and cultural context.

Reference are made to the two other Refugee Processing Centers (RPC) in SEA: Galang, Indonesia and Phanat Nikhom, Thailand, but no direct attempt is made to analyze the organizational structure and concept of the cultural orientation program of these implementing agencies. However, an ad-hoc analysis is done on the results of their training system culminating in staff and refugee student learning.

This study does not attempt to account for the cultural orientation adjustment of Southeast Asian refugees to the U.S. before 1980 that did not participate in the cultural orientation program at one of the RPC's in SEA (Ranard and Pfleger, 1995).

The time frame for cultural orientation and resettlement process for refugees was approximately 18 months, 6 months in PRPC, or less in "special cases" and 12 months in the U.S.

This analysis does at stages involve itself in the legal system (Philippines and U.S.) for treatment of issues that may or may not be bound by the letter of the law i.e., "international law" and U.S. foreign policy.

Rationale

The purpose of this study is to expand the present body of knowledge about how overseas refugee resettlement education is conducted. Its focus is education for living in a multi-ethnic society. The fact that existing literature in this area primarily reflects the Anglo-American perspective, consequently, tending to make it "one-sided," so much so that this has led to the often misguided impression on the part of refugees destined for resettlement in America that the only legitimate cultural perspective of America is that of Anglo-Americans. From the point of view of a non-white American, overseas refugee cultural orientation does not do enough in the area of raising consciousness on some of those vexing and unresolved social issues of American life.

The need for Americans to endeavor to find the solutions to some of these problems is only second to the more important realization that we must share candidly with refugees what in fact some of these problems are.

It is postulated in this work that cultural orientation abroad be expanded to include a more holistic perspective of American culture and society, which is multi-cultural, thereby, also benefitting Southeast Asian refugees resettling in America in their adjustment process.

Not long ago, the U.S. Commission on Civil Rights undertook an investigation: Recent Activities Against Citizens and Residents of Asian Decent (1986) to try and explain why the level of violence targeted at Southeast Asians in particular, and Asians in general, was on the increase. It was suspected that, in part, "poor" race relations between Indochinese and American minority groups was a contributing cause. By no means should overseas refugee cultural orientation be thought of as the latest panacea for fostering racial understanding of American minority groups (Brimelow, 1995).

Nevertheless, the question of what refugees from Southeast Asia have been informed about race relations and existing ethnic strife in America and some of the causes for it, seems to be a cogent question.

Current information relative to continued project funding and the competition existing between stateside and overseas refugee projects to get funding, suggests that, in order for overseas projects such as the International Catholic Migration Commission to remain a viable project for funding consideration, it must begin to assume even more responsibility for cultural orientation issues traditionally handled by stateside agencies. Moreover, as federal funding is being reduced, the ones which are funded will be expected to pick-up where these projects have left off. Not only will they do this, but also point out the fact that because they are overseas, their project is more cost-effective due to access to "cheap" labor (Morgan, 1995). Suffice to say, the question of overseas Refugee Processing Centers (RPC) implementing agencies moving to better meet the need for cultural orientation is a simple matter of project survival. This dissertation serves as an outline of the central issues and concerns of American cultural orientation, and that the work be part of any analysis of the RPC cultural orientation education, present and future.

Methodology

A comprehensive analysis was done on data from field surveys and studies conducted by the training system of the International Catholic Migration Commission in Bataan, Philippines concerning the conceptualization and implementation of Indochinese refugee American cultural orientation and concerns related to the staff, teachers and students. Research data used covered 1980 when the program started until its closure in 1995 (Ranard and Pfleger, 1995).

Content analysis was done on the following Indochinese refugee publications of the Center for Applied Linguistics: The Journal (1981 to 1983), Passage: A Journal of Refugee Education (1985 to 1988), Information Update (1985 to 1988) and In America: Perspectives on Refugee Resettlement (1988 to 1991). This literature served as a primary resource and means for U.S. funded overseas implementing agencies to "share and exchange" information among persons involved in refugee education and resettlement.

The following types of articles comprise the main part of the journals:

- Theoretical constructs related to refugee education in Southeast Asia, Africa and Europe in the training sites of programs.
- Descriptions of projects and activities related to refugee education.
- Practical teaching, training methods and techniques.
- Reviews of books, articles, reports and audio-visual materials relevant to refugee education.
- Photographs illustrating aspects of the educational program and refugee culture.

Further examination was done on field consultant reports, their criticisms and recommendations about the program and the setting, the Philippine Refugee Processing Center.

Personal interviews were conducted by the author with ICMC/ Philippine and PRPC staff, refugees, many other people involved in refugee affairs, such as, the Bureau for Refugee Programs, U.S. Department of State, the U.S. Refugee Coordinator, Vietnam Veterans, international relief agencies, both in the Philippines and the U.S.

The "official" policies and mandates analyzed were the U.S. Department of State / ICMC Philippines Cooperative Agreement and the Republic of the Philippines Government / ICMC Geneva Cooperative Agreement.

Researcher Objectivity

The researcher relocated his residence from the PRPC site to the nearby community of Morong, Bataan from 1981 to 1990. This was done for the purpose of being able to establish and claim objectivity over the field investigation.

During periods of the field research, language translators and interpreters from the respective refugee groups (Vietnamese, Cambodian and Laotian) assisted the researcher.

Intuitive Speculation

In some instances where previously cited methods and instruments did not allow for sufficient testing of "assumptions" or in combination with methods and instruments, intuitive speculation was used to draw conclusions.

Statistical Measurement

To consider answers to questions having to do with qualitative outcomes of instructional program activities, measurement instruments used by others (ICMC/Philippines, Department of State, Center for Applied Linguistics and RMC Research Corporation) were collected and ad hoc analysis conducted.

CHAPTER II

Introduction

I couldn't hold my tears. The moment was wonderful but very sad. I was wishing I could a miracle to have my relatives and friends come along.

A refugee at the transit center in Bangkok

1975 through 1979 is recorded as the period that the plight of the Indochinese refugee came publicly to the attention of the Western world, especially the United States (St. Cartmail, 1983; Vicery, 1984). From Mainland Southeast Asia (SEA) and Indochina (Vietnam, Cambodia and Laos) (see map) millions of inhabitants fled for their lives as the grip of communism took hold of their homeland. So desperate was this flight that people were moved to the point of trying to escape in overcrowded fishing boats attempting to cross the treacherous waters of the South China Sea. Worse yet was the harrowing passage which had to first be made through the Gulf of Thailand where pirate vessels patrolled (see map), waiting for their "defenseless" pray. This human spectacle so horrified the international community that demands were advance by concerned people around the world that something be done to stop this carnage.

Two immediate measures to counter this came into effect (U.S. Department of State, 1985); the United Nations High Commissioner for Refugees (UNHCR) on behalf of the United Nations signed an agreement with the Socialist Republic of Vietnam creating the Orderly Departure Program (ODP) from Vietnam (Migration and Refugee

Service, 1986). The ODP provided a safe, legal means of departure from Vietnam as an alternative to the dangerous escape in small boats. And in 1980 the United States took the initiative along with UNHCR to formulate and implement the Anti-Piracy and Rescue-at-sea Program.[1]

In the fall of Phnom Penh, Cambodia a violent and no less sensational case, it has been estimated that one-third of the population was slaughtered and millions of people were routed from the city (Ngo and Warner, 1987; Vicery, 1984) without food, water or medical supplies and directed by the Communists to resettle in work camps in the deforested countryside. Many of the people saw this as being a life or death struggle and found a way to escape the plight of a work camp. Much like the boat people, the Cambodian understood that this act to be free, to seek a better life would not be without sacrifice. Some did not survive the perilous journey to safety; some disappeared never to be seen or heard from again, and all who survived this journey would remember the passage for the rest of their days.

The arrival at a temporary haven in a first asylum country (as designated by the UNHCR) culminated in the mandatory screening process (Barr, 1987; IRAC, 1988) to "legally" qualify for refugee status. Once this process has begun, the vast majority of refugees find out for the first time what it means to negotiate in the maze of a Western "bureaucracy" and to feel powerless in the process. Because of the legal aspects of this process and the speed with which the wheels of a bureaucracy turn, it is not unusual for complete processing for refugee status to take anywhere from six months to five years (Knox, 1981) or sometimes longer. Prior to 1980, there existed no clear-cut and uniform processing structure at the first asylum refugee camps throughout Southeast Asia.

Once a refugee qualified for resettlement in a Western country (America, Canada, Norway and France — to name a few — he was sent to one of three regional refugee processing centers (RPC's): Bataan, Philippines, Galang, Indonesia and Phanat Nikhom, Thailand. There they were given medical care, screening, and language and cultural orientation training (ICMC, 1986 (c);

1 In 1981, 1,444 attacks on refugee boats were reported in the Gulf of Thailand and nearby waters according to the United Nations refugee agency. Of the 71,667 people known to have fled Vietnam that year 961 were reported killed, 257 taken hostage and 857 women said they had been raped. As late as 1989, 762 Vietnamese or Cambodian refugees were reported killed or missing at sea (Crossette, 1992).

International Red Cross, 1990). The first Southeast Asian refugee wave which had a direct impact on American refugee resettlement occurred in 1975 (Karnow, 1992). To be able to gain further insight into what these refugees were like and the nature of their experience at the refugee camps, two dynamics are worth noting: first, was their social and economic status; the first wave of Indochinese refugees were primarily composed of refugees possessing a significant amount of formal education and/or specialized skills as well as a reasonably good command of either English or French, sometimes both. One characteristic which most of these refugees had in common was the "close working contact" they had with Westerners before the demise of their own non-Communist government (Webb, 1992). This was also a factor in their having to flee from their country after it fell to the Communist. These were "professionals,"[2] coming from the top echelons of society: doctors, senior government officials, lawyers, engineers, professors, (people with "CIA" involvement) and other highly skilled persons (Burns, 1991). Another common trait was their tendency to come from urban areas which lent them a certain urban sophistication.

The second dynamic was their knowledge of a Western language and cross-cultural orientation. For this reason, there was little need for first asylum refugee camps to engage in language and cultural orientation training. Another major consideration in the first wave of Indochinese refugees was their close and "verifiable" (Appendix C) working relationship with the American government. Subsequently, the duration of time they had to "wait" in the refugee camp was far shorter compared with other refugees that could not easily establish a past working relationship with a Western government. The specific U.S. immigration provisions which applied to them set forth that "priority case (were) based either on family ties in the U.S. or employed with an American Government or with a private American firm" (Barr, 1987).

The resettlement process in America for those refugees that were part of the first wave was, considered by private social service agencies and government policy-makers to be, by and large, successful, given the majority of these refugees were able to re-establish themselves in American society and were leading "self-sufficient" and "productive"

2 "Almost half had college degrees and had studies in the United States" (Karnow, 1992).

lives (Hu, 1989; St. Cartmail, 1983). By late 1979, this "first-wave" population dwindled from the RPC roster and slowly took on a new and different profile. During this period, the processing by Western country refugee agencies became noticeably slower as a result of the tremendous backlog of persons applying for refugee resettlement status. One of the first salient characteristics noted in this new clientele was their apparent lack of formal education (Karnow, 1992), skill training or the ability to speak or comprehend a Western language. Taken from the standpoint of processing refugee applicants, this meant processing could only go forward after securing additional language translators and interpreters.

One negative side-effect that came to be part of this experience was the refugee camp itself. The first asylum camp came to be a place where one's life was literally put on hold. The refugee was placed in a situation of limbo where he did not know with any certainty if he would be accepted by a country for resettlement, or when the decision would arrive (Knox, 1981; Ngo and Warner, 1987).

Throughout the 1980's and 1990's journalists representing a host of different countries visited some of the well-known refugee camps in Southeast Asia: Kao-I-Dang, Ben Vinai, Pulao Bidung Island, Malaysia, Chiang Khong, Ban Nam Yao and Sa Kaeo, and reported to readers their perception of what life was like for the refugees there.

These reporters described the seeming endless state of despair; reflective of the day-to-day life of a first asylum camp (IRAC, 1988; Refugees, 1989). It was a place where if one had the strength, and courage, he could dare to hope for the chance of being chosen as a "refugee" to start a new and different life with the realization that this hope could well be years in the making. While one was waiting for word, the asylum camp was a place where the survival alone can be harsh and glaring (International Red Cross, 1990). First asylum refugee camps are under the auspices of the (UNHCR) and are supposed to be recognized as occupying a "safe zone" for refugees. In the case of Thailand (Ngo and Warner, 1987; Robinson, 1987; Richburg, 1989) this was not the reality. Thai first asylum camps near the Thai/Cambodia border had come under artillery bombardment from hostile forces resulting in many refugee fatalities ("A New Refugee Dilemma," 1989). In one such instance, this was "deliberately" done by Thai military forces to dislodge suspected Khmer Rouge guerrilla fighters that had infiltrated the camp. Little wonder that the results of the minimal formal education offered to the refugees was negligible when compared with the other more immediate pressures the refugee had to endure.

The signing in 1980 of the Refugee Act into American law proved to have far-reaching ramifications for the DOS/Bureau of Refugee Programs (Tollefson, 1989 (a); Zucker and Zucker, 1987). This set the direction of American policy, domestic and foreign, with respect to the nature of human services that would be rendered to refugees destined for resettlement in the U.S. This led to the creation of the Refugee Processing Center's (RPC's) in SEA, intended to provide refugees with language and cultural orientation training. The thinking on the part of DOS was for refugees with lower level occupations, skills and English language proficiency would benefit "measurably" from a five-month intensive education program prior to their entering the U.S. (Morgan, 1985 (b); 1995; RMC, 1984). The processing centers were originally set up in three locations throughout the region: Galang, Indonesia, Phanat Nikhom, Thailand; and Bataan, Philippines.

> One of these programs (was) the ICMC Training Program in Morong, Bataan, Philippines, preparing Indochinese refugees for their first six months of resettlement through English as a Second Language (ESL), Cultural Orientation (CO) and Work Orientation (WO) at the largest refugee processing center in the region (Morgan, 1985 (b), p. 6).

It was required (Morgan, 1985 (b)) that RPC's in SEA conform to regional instructional competencies for all refugee students: students from the region would cover the same regional competencies. There was provided latitude to each RPC site as to how this could best be pedagogically and schematically achieved.

The development of the learner's competencies list was developed by a task force composed of instructional staff from the implementing agencies (Blume, 1987; Tollefson, 1986; 1989 (a)) in addition to instructional support and expertise provided by the Center for Applied Linguistics (CAL). From this list of competencies (Appendix E) it is possible to get a better idea of the nature of language and cultural orientation of the learner, and more importantly, what "assumptions" (Tollefson, 1989 (a)) refugee educators and administrators had about what the refugee needed to be able to make a positive adjustment to life in the U.S. (Ascher, 1985).

The psychological as well as physical move of the refugee from a first asylum camp to a processing center is of significance. For one, it is the long awaited answer to the question (International Red Cross, 1990): When will this journey of flight end? To receive confirmation for overseas resettlement processing meant that there was now, "light at the end of the tunnel." For the vast majority of refugees, psychologically, this high point was perceived and taken to mean that one had "arrived" for the first time at the threshold. Many of them could already begin to feel what it must be like to live in a free and open society. The responsibility they were about to undertake was often times forgotten or overlooked when thinking glorious thoughts of what it must be like to be a free human being.

Life in the first asylum camps has been characterized as static and depressing (Knox, 1981; Robinson, 1987; Refugees, 1989). The reason being: the refugee's psychological and physical constitution was already overtaxed with one primary concern, how to hold on and survive one more day. This is how stark and real the instability of the environment could be. The first asylum refugee experience may be thought of as, primarily experienced at the primal level of human existence.[3] Transferring to a processing center can be thought of in terms of "moving up" the ladder of higher order needs as described in the treatise Hierarchy of Needs (Maslow, 1970). To be sure, the refugee not missing the significance of this good fortune, plans for a warm and festive "thanksgiving." This is the time when the refugee can become confused and overwhelmed; he isn't sure if he wants to laugh or cry. Another painful step in moving to another refugee camp, but this time, getting nearer to a place where one will be physically safe, have enough food to eat, adequate hospital care (Felsman, et al, 1989); a place without fear of religious persecution; and a place where he can receive some education that will prepare him for life in a modern, free, complex — and mixed race — society (Kearny, Kearny and Crandall, 1984).

By virtue of my work experience for nine and a half years in service to the refugee cause, "I can personally attest to the refugee

3 The (PBS) documentary Situation Zero is a moving account of a typical day in a Cambodians life-reflects conditions in refugee camps along the Thai-Cambodian border (International Red Cross, 1990).

experience at the Philippine Refugee Processing Center (PRPC)." For many refugees PRPC became the place where one could reach out to others and communicate once again openly about what they thought, felt and hoped. Once the reality of becoming a temporary resident at the PRPC had time to set in, the refugee would have acquired an insatiable appetite for asking every kind of question imaginable.

There is the other side to the refugee experience at a processing center. Frequently, the physical move from Indochina to SEA is not without its mental and emotional upset. Indeed, in some cases the experience is traumatic (Baker, et al, 1983). It was not that uncommon for the first asylum experience to mean having had buried a loved one or dear friend (Refugees, 1989) and now the time had come to move on. Some others may again have had to come to grips with the fact that they had lost track of loved ones and friends, and by moving farther away, the chances for finding their whereabouts seemingly became even more remote. Just as there was to be found the reality of death in the first asylum camp, there was also the spectacle of new life unfolding: babies born in a refugee camp. Suffice to say, this was equally true for the RPC's.[4] This reality was painful as it was joyous!

By design, the RPC acted as a "quasi-educational" institution (Tollefson, 1989 (a)) addressing the basic educational and cultural needs of refugees preparing to enter American society. The fact that refugee overseas resettlement education was done in a country other than America and used foreign teachers to teach about American culture made the "challenge" of presenting it to students all the more formidable a task (Blassingame, 1984; 1987; Maciel, 1985; Mydans, 1988; Martin, 1986; Redding, 1985; Thang, 1987; Verzosa, 1988; White, 1988).

The fact that the American staff working within RPC's in general and ICMC/ Philippines in particular held the key positions lent credence to the idea that Americans were the one responsible for making the program work (ICMC, 1987 (d); Tollefson, 1989 (a). Thereafter, at every opportunity, Americans in this setting were performing two basic and important functions relative to helping refugees better understand American culture (Kearny, Kearny and Crandall, 1984): First, actively fostering and promoting an awareness

4 Since 1985 twelve (12) babies had been born at the PRPC hospital (Life, 1989); less to mention the births that the author places in the hundreds, which have taken place in the PRPC while "waiting" for a vehicle to transport a pregnant mother to the hospital.

for multi-ethnicity within the RPC milieu in the "American" sense of a pluralistic and racially mixed community. Secondly, the Americans had to shoulder responsibility for using the milieu for further sensitizing refugees to the ethnical and moral issues of democratic life, taking particular care to "demonstrate" how concepts like freedom, equality, cultural sensitivity and cooperative living work in principle and action.

In the end, host country, American and other expatriate instructional staff combined within the cultural orientation program and endeavored to bring the SEA refugees to terms with the American way of live before setting out on the final leg of their journey.

Environment and Setting

I could see that my significance as an individual was small . . . . I had become, whether I liked it or not, a symbol representing [my] people . . . . I could [not] run away from this situation.

Marian Anderson

The Philippine Refugee Processing Center (PRPC) was three hours northwest of Manila located on a mountain ridge overlooking the South China Sea (PRPC, 1988). Many visitors to the PRPC were taken by its resemblance to a suburban college or university campus. In the words of Dr. Andrea Van Chau, ICMC/Geneva Secretary General: "The camp gave me a feeling of a village — even a college campus" (Chau, 1988). The PRPC could accommodate a refugee population of seventeen thousand (17,000) (Burns, 1991; Lee, 1989; Philippine Refugee Processing Center, 1988), in addition to some three thousand three hundred (3,300) resident staff (and in some cases their families) from the various agencies operating at the center that in some manner served the needs of refugees.

Source: PRPC, 1988.

The agencies were: Adventist Development Relief Agency, Community Mental Health Service (CMHS), Intergovernmental Committee for Migration (ICM), International Catholic Migration Commission (ICMC), Japanese Overseas Corps of Volunteers (JOCV), Joint Voluntary Agencies (JVA),[5] Mormon Christian Services, Norwegian Government, Philippine Baptist Refugee Ministries (PBRM), Philippine National Red Cross, Philippine Refugee Processing Center (PRPC), Rotary International, Salvation Army, United Nations High Commissioner for Refugees (UNHCR),Welfare Agency of the

5 JVA was also operated by ICMC under another Cooperative Agreement with the Bureau for Refugee Programs, U.S. Department of State.

Archdiocese of Manila, and the World Relief Corporation (WRC) (PRPC, 1988). The PRPC could be further described as a "self-contained" community, in that, one's essential needs could be met without leaving the setting (Ranard and Pfleger, 1995).

The ICMC map of the PRPC (see Map 1) does not adequately reflect some essential features of the PRPC setting (as true for the PRPC map developed by the PRPC), (Appendix D). To make up for this, supplemental information is provided: the numbers 1-10 in the ICMC map represent refugee neighborhoods. In the back of neighborhood four (4), in the upper right-hand corner of the map is a clear water mountain stream that was a popular spot for hiking, picnic, swimming and fishing for residents of the camp; it used to be the home of the relocated Negrito tribe, who lives in the mountains of the Philippines (Harrison, 1987 (a)). Between refugee neighborhood seven (7), dormitories and the pre-employment center[6] were six (6) helicopter landing pads used for visiting dignitaries and government officials. There was a power generation station less than two hundred yards inside of the PRPC beyond the main checkpoint which supplied emergency power to the site when public power was interrupted, resulting in either a brownout or blackout. This was a common occurrence during the rainy season from June to December. Located in neighborhood eight (8) was the PRPC cemetery.

With the exception of the Indochinese refugees, Japanese and Filipino staff in residence at the center, most recognized PRPC as a work haven for members of the white race (Taneda, 1985). Of the approximately two hundred American, Canadian, British, German, French, Australian, New Zealander and Norwegian, and other European countries represented, only three minorities- of-color could be distinguished in the PRPC setting (ICMC, 1986a). Throughout the history of the PRPC, countless stories of human interest describing the physical setting and environment were written by national and international newspapers and magazines: Chicago Tribune, Christian Science Monitor, International Herald Tribune, Life, Manila Bulletin, Newsweek, New York Times, Philippine Star, Refugee Magazines, San Francisco Chronicle, U.S. News and World Report, and USA Today, to name a few. Not one of these articles made reference to the almost complete absence of "non-white" Westerners in a place whose mission it was to prepare Southeast Asian (SEA) refugees for a positive

6 In 1986 the Pre-employment Training Program was renamed Work Orientation Program (Gilson, 1987).

adjustment to life in a multi-ethnic society as America (ICMC, 1984 (b); Morgan, 1995).

However, for an African-American like Blassingame, his experience of being swamped by refugees for plain curiosity, to touch his dark skin, to hear him speak English, and answer their questions, the encounter was challenging. For the refugee, to see and come close to an Afro-American, was a rarity, not a common experience (Conner, 1991; Kern, 1991). Ironically, upon resettlement in America, most likely they would become neighbors (Wilson, 1987).

To the inhabitants of PRPC, there was little, if any, consensus of what culture the PRPC reflected. The Americans claimed the environment did not reflect American culture (Crisfield and Redding, 1983; Kearny, Kearny and Crandall, 1984). The Filipinos said, it did not reflect Filipino culture. The refugees were, nevertheless, informed that they were observing and experiencing, in their immediate environment, a taste of American culture (Podlaski, 1989). Generally, they believed that by having arrived at the PRPC, after years of being processed in the asylum camps of Thailand and Indonesia, they had only advanced their refugee status to the highest possible degree. The staff resident population of the PRPC shared this unique living situation in PRPC as having become members of a culture that could best be described and characterized as <u>refugee</u> culture (Ranard and Pfleger, 1995).

The PRPC had the appearance of being an orderly run place with all inhabitants aware of the rules. Upon the entrance of the camp, the first refugee neighborhood (seven), a large sign listed the PRPC code of behavior for refugees, as well as corresponding penalties for each code violation (PRPC, 1988). Much like people to be found in any community, refugees were, by-in-large, law- abiding. It was true, some of the codes of behavior were "new" and "strange" to the refugees; they were, however, prepared to go along with them, simply to guarantee that they would not harm their chances of going to America at the end of their five-month training.

There were two (2) pervasive realities of life at PRPC that all employees and residents in their own individual way had to come to terms with. One was that it was a highly artificial situation to bring about certain elements together for the purpose of refugee orientation that would not otherwise had evolved on its own (<u>Pacific Stars and Stripes</u>, 1988). Two was the fact that PRPC/ICMC being the largest project of its kind in the world (Burr, 1987) made it a "model" (Sison, 1988) and showpiece that attracted the attention of important people and organizations from around the world. People that resided there, could do little to escape the fact that they lived in a "fish bowl" type of existence, always being looked at from the outside.

Physical Configuration

To a number of staff working and residing at the PRPC, there invariably came a time when one stopped to wonder: What were the architects of the physical setting ultimately out to achieve (Ranard and Pfleger, 1995; Tollefson, 1989 (a))? Was there a comprehension and appreciation for the fact that the physical setting would either complement or detract from the mission and objective of preparing SEA refugees for initial resettlement-in America? In fact, when the PRPC was initially constructed in 1979, there was no "master plan" for a refugee processing and education site (Burr, 1987). At that time, the PRPC was viewed as a short-term project with a future in doubt. This brought about a physical design that was at best, "tentative." Apparently, because the idea of constructing the Refugee Processing Center (RPC) (originally, three: Galang, Indonesia, Phanat, Nikhom, Thailand and Bataan, Philippines) in SEA was essentially "temporary," it gave way to using low-cost building materials, such as asbestos (CAL, 1983 (a)), which was known to be carcinogenic.

The construction of the PRPC had been, from its inception to 1988 an ongoing process which was halted as a result of the Bureau for Refugee Programs, U.S. Department of State (DOS), budget cut[7] to ICMC (ICMC, 1988 (b)). The history of construction of PRPC begun with the construction of the building structures in Phase I: the PRPC/ICMC Administrative Area in January 1980 (Map 2). At that point in time, the operation was much smaller than in the mid and late eighties. In the beginning, no one really knew the volume of Indochinese

7 The budget cut to ICMC was part of across-the-board cuts to all refugee programs (domestic and international) funded by the U.S. government.

refugees fleeing Indochina,[8] and the commitment on the part of the U.S. government to respond to this crisis. Once the U.S. government made its position publicly known, it became necessary to expand the PRPC site to accommodate, a maximum of seventeen thousand (17,000)[9] SEA refugees (Burns, 1991). By 1980, Phase II and the Pre-Employment Training (PET) compound were completed. By 1985 the Preparation for American School System (PASS) complex was completed (Map 4). By 1986 PRPC had become so sprawling and populated that it had three bus transportation systems, one operated by ICMC, another by World Relief, and the other by PRPC, to move refugees, staff and supplies between Phase I and II and between Manila and Bataan.

Classrooms and refugee billets where the refugees lived while at the PRPC as stated in map 3 and 4, were located in "refugee neighborhoods." On both sides of the classrooms in refugee neighborhoods were asbestos billets in which the refugees lived, as well as the outside bathroom stalls. Map 1 and 4 indicate that refugee neighborhood seven (7) was in close proximity to the ICMC staff dormitory area, being practically joined together.

The next prominent feature of the setting was the school. In June 1988, there were approximately three hundred classrooms operated by ICMC which could be found all over the PRPC. Only two physical configurations, the PASS complex (Map 4) and the Work Orientation compound (previously PET Center) (Map 5) conformed to what most people would regard as a "traditional" school set-up.

Most conventional and some "non-traditional" school facilities have a teachers' conference room, where teachers are able to prepare lessons, go over notes and confer with fellow teachers. Of the five instructional programs (Work Orientation, WO, Cultural Orientation, CO, Preparation for American School System, PASS; English-as-a Second Language, ESL; and Assistant Teacher Paraprofessional Program, ATPTP), only two had a teachers' conference room facilities. The final result of this was teachers had little choice but to use their dormitory as the venue for preparing lessons for the class. Given the physical reality of the living situation in the dormitories, the teachers were forced to make the best of a bad situation.

---

8 In 1979, in a position paper the Indochina Refugee Action Center (IRAC) stated that, "at least 1 million refugees had begun fleeing Indochina and 2 - 3 million more could be expected. . ." (Harmon, 1995).

9 The author was not been able to establish why 17,000 capacity was settled on.

Staff Living Accommodations

A teacher shared a small dormitory with thirteen other ICMC staff members below the job level of Deputy Program Officer. Each dormitory had one large dining room table, good for a maximum of eight persons; two refrigerators; two bathrooms; two burner hot plates; and a kerosene stove (in the event of an electrical blackout). Each room had one portable fan, two small desks, and two single beds. The desk in the dormitory room was so small that the teacher and other instructional staff members often had to use the kitchen table which could accommodate all of the instructional materials that they had to prepare for class. This resulted in problems when a resident of the dorm wished to use the dining table for its original purpose. There was the constant problem of noise, be it someone down the hall playing the radio too loud and/or watching TV. Any way one chose to look at the problem, the teacher was at a loss, and went out to look for a quiet and secluded place to get some work done.

Some of the more obvious and long standing complaints of the dorm residents was. The rooms were too small for one person,[10] let alone "officially" designating it for two. The dormitory living situation (see Map 6) did not adequately allow for one to have a sense of privacy. Most of the problems that developed at the dorm level could often be attributed to the shortcomings in the building design.

Apart from the dormitories being built with asbestos materials (later refurbished with other more acceptable building materials), they were not built with any regard for reducing the noise level to any acceptable degree. Any resident of a dormitory, at anytime of the day

10 As an Instructional teacher, the author shared a dorm room for (28) days before moving to Morong because it was not large enough to accommodate his personal possessions; which was all of two medium sized trunks.

or night, without any effort on their part, could hear the conversation going on next door.

For supervisors who were married, with or without children, and had enough seniority, were entitled to a small, one-room apartment, referred to as married couples dorm. Staff in this category had the benefit of a private bathroom, refrigerator, and outdoor patio.

For positions above supervisory level, other living arrangements prevailed (ICMC, 1987b; Tollefson, 1989 (a)). Single trainers and deputy program officers were provided a dorm room for themselves. Unlike the supervisors below them in job level, but who were married, they did not get the benefit of having a private bathroom and refrigerator.

At the program officer level, one or two bedroom housing (depending on the number and presence of immediate dependents) was provided in another area of the camp, a short distance away from the staff dormitory. It was a widely held belief by the instructional staff that this should have been the model for dorms at the teacher, supervisor, trainer, and deputy program officer levels.

Persons in senior management positions occupied housing in yet another area of the PRPC and, unlike the rest of the housing configuration, this was regarded as American size and furnished with "hot" running water and in-camp telephone.[11] Senior management personnel was provided with private staff vehicles.

Ironically, as the need for staff housing continued to grow, it was noted by the ICMC rank-and-file that upper management living quarters continued to get larger, while dormitory living space progressively got smaller. The newly constructed dormitories were smaller in size than the older dorms, while the number of residents in the dorm remained the same.

The psychological state of those staff living in cramped dormitories and married dorms was noticeably different from staff in higher management (Tollefson, 1989 (a)). Not surprising, there existed much more interpersonal conflicts at the dormitory level. Approximately, a third of the staff living in the dorms were married (ICMC, 1988b); but because they could not bring their dependents to camp to live with them, there existed a "preoccupation" with family affairs back home. One manifestation of this was reflected in the number of absences from work.

11 The telephone rarely worked: it seemed more of a status symbol than anything else.

The idea and concept of privacy in the staff dormitory living area was almost non-existent, given the structure and arrangement of the living environment. This situation, by virtue of culture (Andres, 1981; 1985) was more problematic for Americans (Cristfield and Redding, 1983; Kearny, Kearny and Crandall, 1984) and other Westerners. The reality of life in the dormitory had often been referred to as dismal. For example, what do you do when you go to the dormitory refrigerator to get a cold drink of water at 2:45 A.M. from your container that had your name boldly written on it and found it empty. You know you filled the container before you went to bed. But, there is a full container of cold water on the side of your empty one and it looks mighty tempting. So, what do you do? (One man's heaven is another man's hell!)

What do you do when your dormmates, three doors down the hall, play their radio loud at 5:00 A.M. almost every morning? You have taken up this matter with the persons in question and the dorm manager and both are of the opinion that what is lacking is "cultural sensitivity" on your part.

You are an American, six feet three inches tall, your bed is five feet eight inches in length. Try and get a good nights sleep — try dreaming you were five feet eight inches tall.

There was to be found ICMC staff that opted for a different living arrangement by residing at their own expense outside of the PRPC. Most could be found living in the seaside hamlet of Morong, Mabayo or Sabang. This small group gave as their main reasons for not staying at the PRPC the premium they placed on the need for being able to separate work from their personal life (Ranard and Pfleger, 1995; Schaffer, 1986), and likewise, being able to secure living space adequate enough to have their family with them. Some lived outside of the camp for the benefit of being able to have privacy and to regain the seemingly lost feeling of independence by not being caught between having to choose between dorm life and the peer pressure that came with it, not to mention the host of other petty aggravations that were part of dorm life. Most had not denied that living at the PRPC was probably, in the long run, safer; however, the "control" that they were able to exert over their lives was worth the risks involved.

Curfew as a Way of Life

The curfew at the PRPC began at 10:00 P.M. when everything in the camp was "officially" closed (ICMC, 1984 (b); Philippine Refugee Processing Center, 1988). The only other exception to this was occasional staff social functions such as a farewell party for an agency head that might warrant an extension of the curfew hour; the lifting of which was at daybreak between 5:30-5:45 A.M. The curfew purportedly made it possible to reasonably insure the physical safety of the PRPC residents and property.

Anyone familiar with a refugee camp and how it was run, would agree that refugees, by the time they reached a Refugee Processing Center (RPC), had learned how to respond to a curfew decree. They were motivated to comply because they did not wish to be involved in activity which could hinder their departure for resettlement.

On the other hand, in the case of PRPC staff, the motivation for compliance to the curfew was altogether different. While after 10:00 P.M. all services and activities came to a close and there was nothing open that the only other place left to go was to one's dormitory or staff house. In reality, this logic fell short for some residents whose compliance was begrudgingly brought about by peer group pressure.

Each staff dormitory had a dorm manager, a teacher or supervisor. The manager's task was to see to the smooth and orderly running of the dormitory. Perfunctory tasks of the manager included: assigning and posting a monthly schedule of whose turn it was to defrost and clean the refrigerator, empty the garbage, clean the bathroom, stove, keep the front and back entrance to the dorm clean, and be the mediator when there were arguments or disagreements between residents and to admonish those who did not comply with the curfew. The dormitory manager was the lone person in the dormitory that held the keys to the front and back doors of the dormitory.

Since better than one-half of the approximately twelve hundred ICMC staff were single and unattached (ICMC, 1988b), some even reported to be on the "lookout" for a soul mate, the closure of PRPC services did not necessarily mean for them that all activity had to come to a stop. These folks had been known to make a last minute stop at the PRPC Guest House and collect a case of cold beer and/or soft drinks and/or whatever else, that would help the evening along and proceed to a friend's dormitory to continue where they left off. This after hours social would go along fine until the time finally came to say "good night." Entry into a dormitory after curfew could be a real headache: the "problem" boiled down to who, besides the dormitory manager would open the door for them. There existed, especially in dormitories where many residents were Filipino, the strong suspicion that a "female" who was not present in the dormitory before curfew was a person of dubious character (Agoncillo and Alfonso, 1960; Cristfield and Redding, 1983). Such a person would eventually be permitted entrance but not without first having to knock on almost all of the residents' windows, and thereby, in the process, getting the definite impression that it would have been easier trying to wake the dead.

Contrary to popular belief, some staff members chose to remain in camp on their week(s) off.[12] Inasmuch as the number of this group was low, some of them lived in the provinces and avoided the expense of travel or short stay in Manila.

The majority of people participated in a massive exodus from the PRPC once every six weeks, which usually meant returning to the province or cities to join relatives and or friends. For the American and other expatriates, this generally meant a chance to travel and see the sights of the Philippines. In some cases, when staff had no clear sense of where they would go on their week(s) off, they simply reasoned that it did not really matter because the bottom line was that any place was better than spending it at PRPC.

As one could imagine, it was not humanly possible to account for the whereabouts of some seven to eight hundred teachers and supervisors when they had time off from work. Nevertheless, it was uncanny that at least half of the staff could be easily located in Manila at three pension houses (Malate, Sorriente's and Santos). The author asked a number of Filipino associates why they thought so many

12 The teachers Needs Assessment Survey (White, 1988) generated comments about the work schedule and how staff spent their time off.

ICMC staff frequented these particular pensions. The response was that they were located in the heart of the metropolis, a short distance from the ICMC administrative office, the restaurant, shopping, and theatre district. Everything that one could possibly want to do was right at his doorstep. More importantly, it was pointed out that since ICMC staff enjoyed a special discount on lodging, it only cost them approximately fifty pesos (the equivalent of $1.75) per day (Soriente's was about double the price) to share a dormitory with three other persons. Another fact was that these two places were clean and well-maintained.

How Time Is Measured

Instructional staff worked a forty-eight (48) hour work week, lasting for six (6) days from Monday to Saturday. At the end of six weeks, the instructional staff was entitled to one week off. At the end of the second six-week stretch, they were entitled to two weeks off. This work time-off scheme by staff was called the "six-one, six-two" schedule.[13] One of the major setbacks to this environment was that there was a heavy emphasis on work, and even when one was not working, it was not easy to get away from the pervasive atmosphere. On the other hand, work was one of the easiest things to do because PRPC did not offer room for much else (White, 1988). The only time when one was clearly separated from work was when they left the setting (Ranard and Pfleger, 1995). ICMC staff, much like refugees, had learned how to master the art of "waiting" and this was usually done by keeping oneself busy. The common notion was that it was possible to measure the time an instructional staff member had been in PRPC since his last week(s) off in a couple of ways that were thought to be fairly reliable: in week five and six, it was purported that a staff person was generally more irritable and short-tempered or indifferent to what was going on around him. Conversely, it was conjectured that the observation of a staff member looking relaxed and refreshed must have meant that he had just recently returned from his week(s) off.

Some staff measured their time by a project or projects they managed to complete, not necessarily directly related to the schedule. They did not measure time with any real sense of urgency but rather productivity. For other instructional staff, the measure of time was connected to the student cycle they happened to be assigned to work

13 February 1989, ICMC instituted a new break schedule called the "static break" 6 - 1 schedule: All staff had a one week break at the end of six weeks. For an overview of problems related to this, see Appendix A: 5 Day Work Week Survey Results.

with. A cycle began when refugees came into PRPC and officially began instruction which would last for a period of five months, followed by graduation exercise which brought the cycle to a close. There was some staff that fell into more than one category of the above, as well as those that measured time with respect to capital investment: How much money they had managed to save in a given amount of time; they were the staff that remained in PRPC on their week(s) off so they could save more money (ICMC, 1988b).

For the majority of refugees that came to the PRPC from first asylum camps in SEA, of which the average waiting time was four years (Nguyen, 1988) before clearance to proceed for final processing to a third country for resettlement, they had long gotten used to the idle existence and state of depression of refugee camp life of "waiting." But the fact that the PRPC did afford them a measurable degree of "freedom" for some social activity, it was not uncommon for refugees to equate the PRPC experience as the first time in a number of years that they had felt what it was like to be free, comparatively speaking. In this context, the special needs of the refugees seemed modest and easy to satisfy. Time was measured, for the most part, from 5:30 A.M. to 9:30 P.M., the curfew hours set for refugees. The greatest social activities they had was going to school, church, recreation-facilities and neighboring to visit other refugees and PRPC residents that had befriended them. Others went ("unauthorized") to the closest cities of Olongapo and Balanga for shopping and/or sightseeing.

Most of all, the reality that they were at the PRPC and in the final stages of ending their journey, one could be sure, they were counting the days when they would leave PRPC for America. At any time, most refugees could tell you in (broken) English when they expected their time to come to say good-bye to friends they have made at the PRPC and at other points along the way. Some refugee with great pain and an aching heart had cause to remember that for someone near and dear to them, time no longer had any earthly meaning because it had carried them beyond. The wish was for time to heal what was left of the broken heart (Baker, et al, 1983).

Stress, Anxiety and Political Unrest

The aftermath of the February 26, 1986 People's Power Revolution, promptly noted internationally as the first "non-violent" revolution of modern times (Mercado, 1986; Project 28 Days, 1986) the hoped-for-era of peace, unity, democracy and stability, only served to confront the citizenry with the fact that the strength of the "new" democratic order would ultimately be judged by how well it withstood deadly opposition[14] from political enemies ("Cory Regime Faces Right, Left Threats," 1989). There were many people that believed that because the PRPC was located in a remote location, the reality of overt warring factions against the government would not make itself known, in any "true to life" manner, save for reading about such events in the newspaper and on the TV.

But on the afternoon of February 15, 1987, residents of PRPC had to deal with the reality that the Municipal Hall of Morong, Bataan located seven kilometers away from PRPC came under siege, "attacked" by suspected elements of the New People's Army (NPA). A fierce fire-fight between government forces and the NPA raged from late afternoon well into the night. It was necessary for a detachment of security forces from the PRPC to assist government forces at the Morong City Hall. If this was not enough to generate attention at the PRPC, a year later, the annual town festival was held in the Morong town square where thousands of people were gathered, including staff and refugees from the camp. Suddenly, without warning, a fire-fight erupted in the middle of the town square between NPA and local government forces. Unlike the first incident, where miraculously, only

14 By December 1989, the Aquino government had survived (7) coup attempts (Stewart, 1989).

minor injuries resulted, this one ended with two dead, and a few others seriously injured. The illustration that PRPC was the safest place one could hope for, was no longer the case.

To be sure, ICMC staff had "personal" concerns stemming from these incidents. In one of the management forum meetings between staff and senior management, a staff member asked the project director what plans ICMC had in the event the PRPC ever came under attack. This was followed by an American staff member wishing to know what the American Embassy in Manila would do to safeguard the American citizens at the camp. Inasmuch as senior management reassured staff that precautionary measures would be taken, this failed to satisfy most of those present. Management suggested to staff that it was just as much their "responsibility," as well as the management's, to be prudent and vigilant so as not to find oneself in the "wrong place at the wrong time." At about this same time, the American Embassy through ICMC began furnishing on a regular basis American employees of ICMC, circulars addressing the political unrest in the Philippines and advising alertness and caution ("U.S. Lists RP Cities Safe for Travel," 1988).

Given the political unrest, remoteness and isolation of PRPC (Tollefson, 1989 (a)) which was previously thought to contain more pluses than minuses, suddenly appeared to have marked disadvantages: there was no telephone communication between Morong and Manila before 1990. The nearest place one could go to make a telephone call was thirty minutes away.[15] Even then, it was heading into rebel territory.

This state of national and individual stress and anxiety brought on by the post-trauma of the People's Power Revolution (Mercado, 1986; Project 28 Days, 1986; Zich, 1986) had not gone without notice by the refugees. It was not uncommon for a refugee student, when things flaired up politically (Lobo and Rodriguez, 1989; "Revolt in the Philippines," 1989; Siytangco, 1989; "Strike Vs. Industrial Pace," 1988), to ask their Filipino teachers to comment on what was happening and what were some of the social forces at work. This was a tough question because the "facts" were not easy to come by. Subsequently, this was to inadvertently place the teacher in a tight

15 Although Subic Navel Base was seven (7) kilometers away from PRPC with telephone facilities (local and international), only authorized persons with passes could enter. According to ICMC, only senior management staff were authorized to have such a pass.

situation. A considerable number of them had not yet figured out in their own minds what was actually happening politically, much less, be in the position to explain it to a student if he was to ask.

To fully comprehend the state of Filipino political affairs was not an easy task (Solidarity Conference, 1987; Zich, 1986). Meanwhile, only one thing seemed to be certain: that no one in the Philippines was that far removed or out-of-touch that he did not feel that political change was anything but a peaceful process, inspite of how much it might have been prayed for.

Two of the undisputed "get-away" places from the immediate environment of the PRPC for staff and refugees was the Morong beach and the Rice Mill Restaurant Inn. The beauty and tranquillity of the beach fronting the South China Sea and the opportunity to gain the (needed) sense of anonymity made Morong a special place. This get-away could do much to invigorate the weary soul and body.

For the PRPC, ICMC and other human services agencies staff, a good number of them would have said that the Rice Mill Restaurant in its own right was an establishment that could not easily be separated from the refugee community (Sales and Cabanes, 1987) by virtue of the fact that it had provided the much needed venue for staff, refugees and visitors to get food to eat and needed "quiet time" to reflect and project the reality of being and striving to serve the refugee cause.

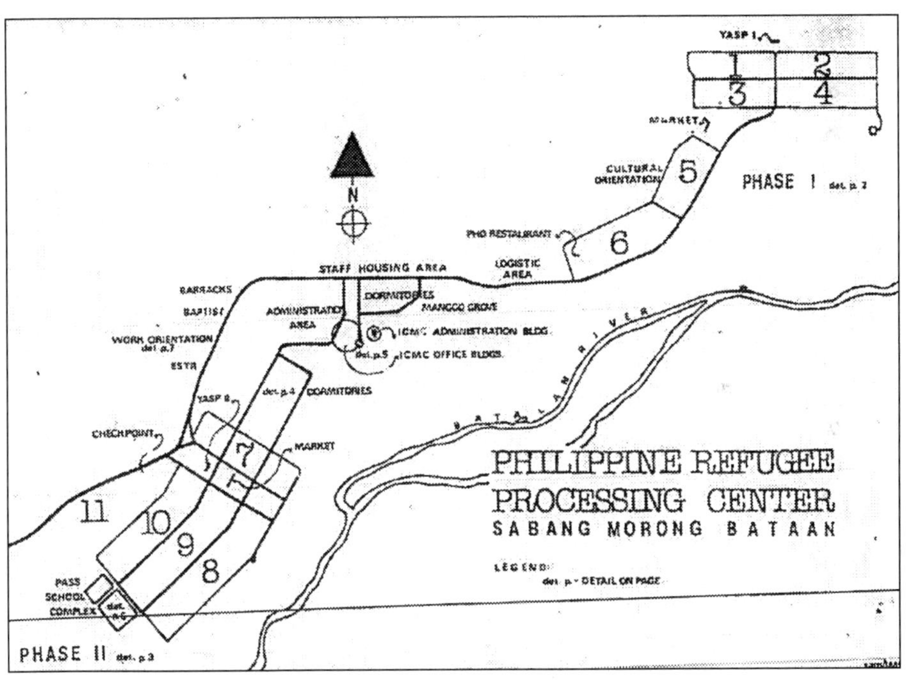

Source: Materials Production Unit, ICMC/Philippines

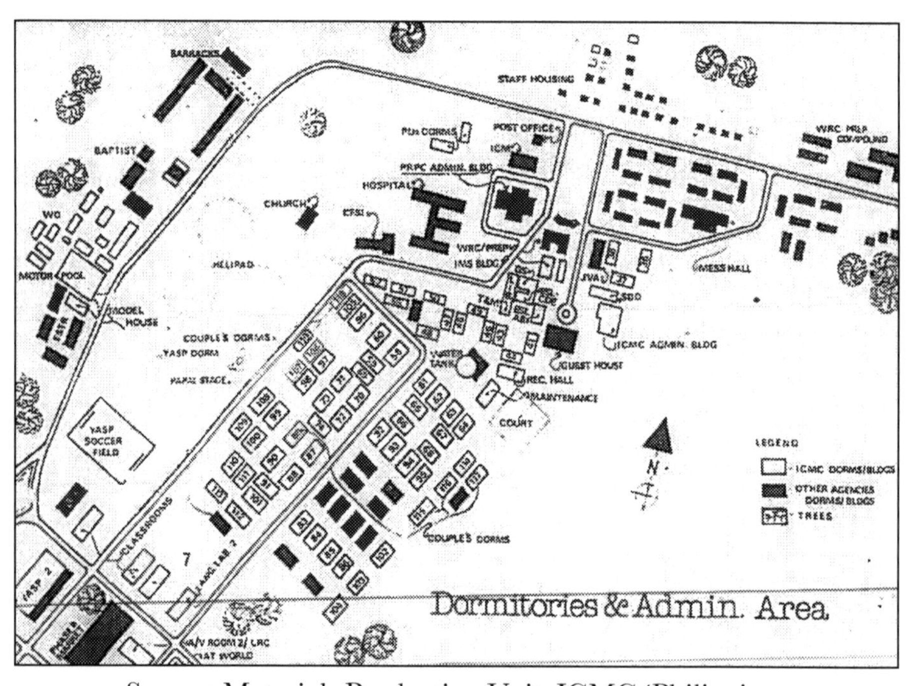

Source: Materials Production Unit, ICMC/Philippines

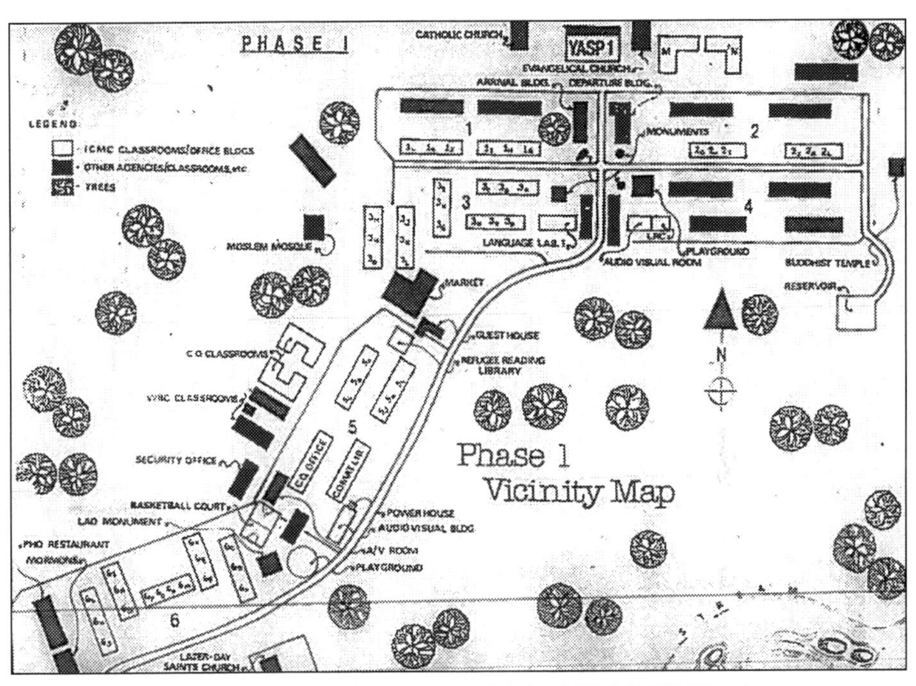

Source: Materials Production Unit, ICMC/Philippines

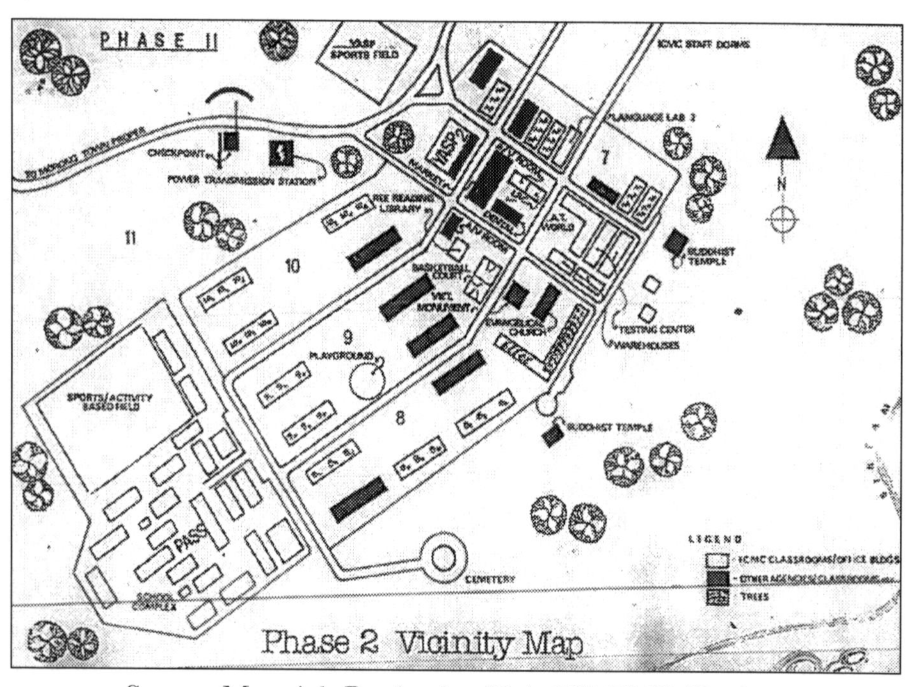

Source: Materials Production Unit, ICMC/Philippines

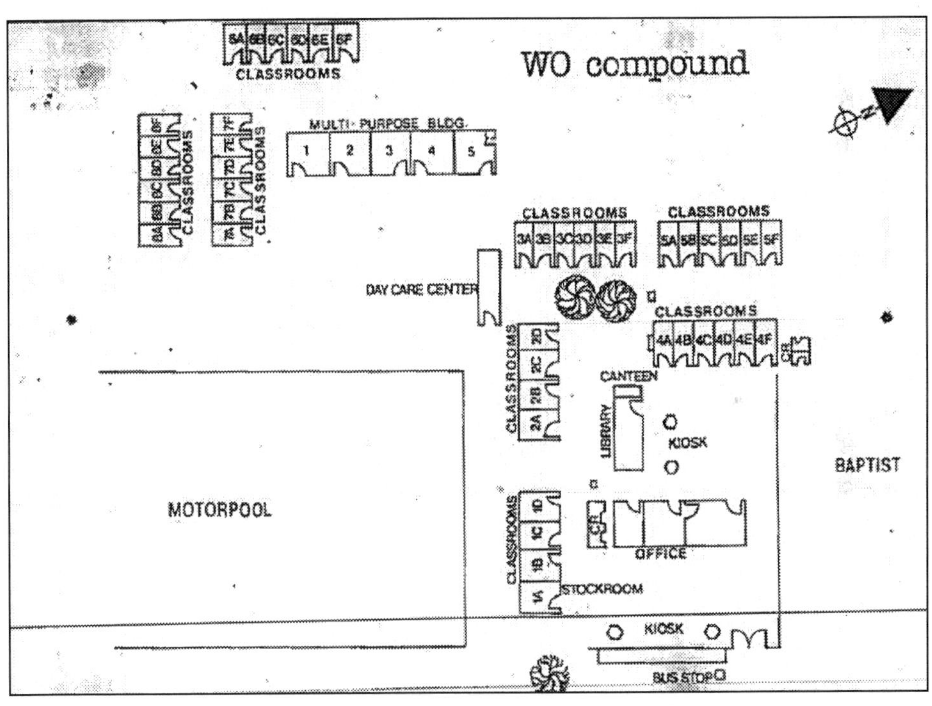

Source: Materials Production Unit, ICMC/Philippines

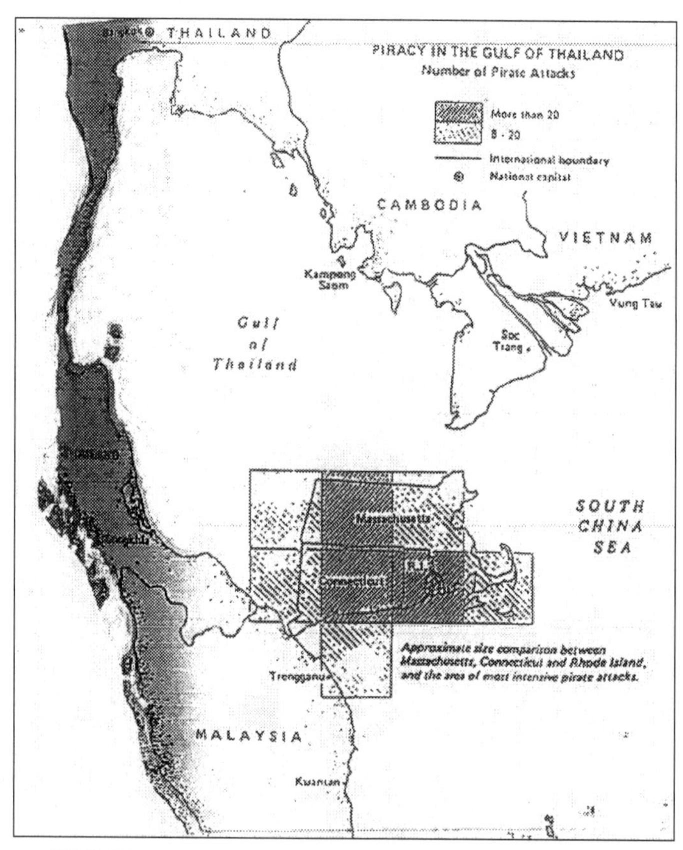

Source: U.S. Department of State, Bureau of Refugee Programs. World Refugee Report, (September 1985).

Source: U.S. Department of State, Bureau of Refugee Programs. World Refugee Report, (September 1985).

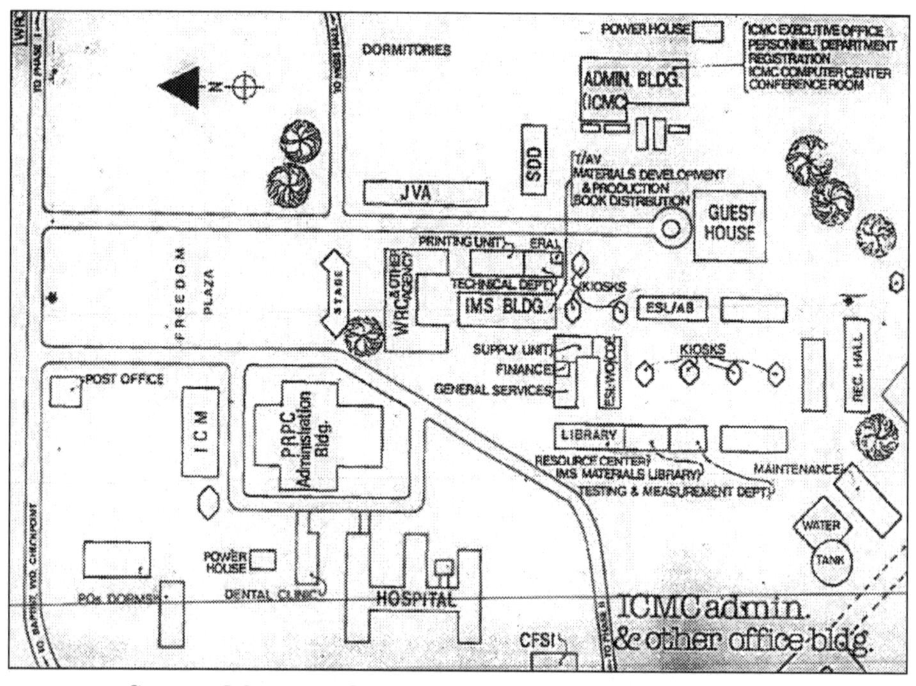

Source: Materials Production Unit, ICMC/Philippines

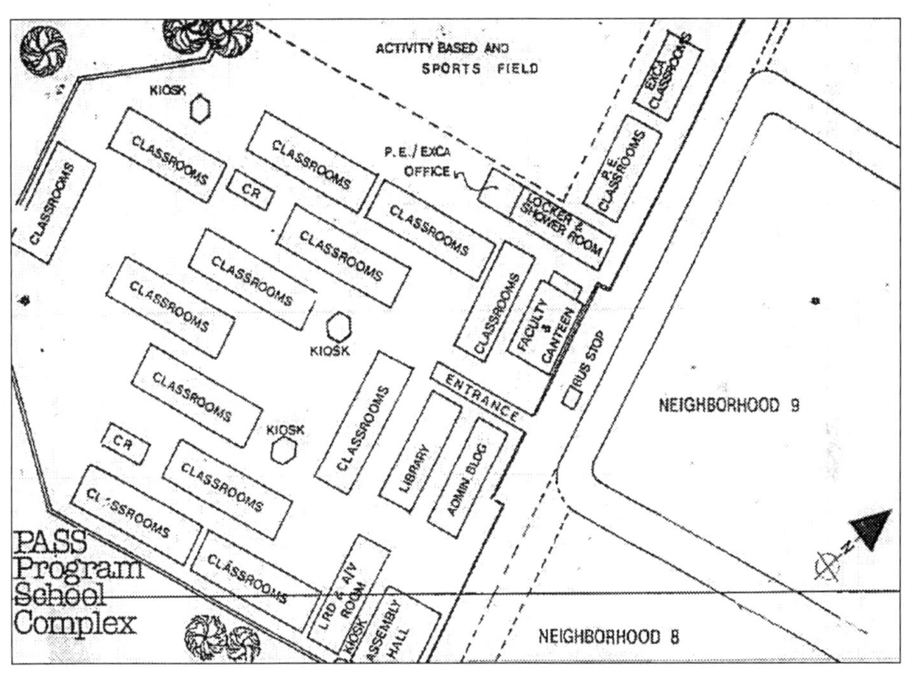

Source: Materials Production Unit, ICMC/Philippines

CHAPTER III

Organizational Structure: Historical Background, Management Style and Issues

From 1980 to 1992, ICMC/Philippines was handled by four (4) project directors, whose respective stewardships were from 1980 - 1984, 1984 - 1985, 1985 - 1987 and 1988 - 1992. As a general manager, each projected his own vision (Blume, 1987) of what needed to be achieved and own distinct management style (Kotter, 1982) that affected the organization and staff. Equally important was the fact that upon arrival, each was met with challenging organizational dynamics already at work.

Next to the project director, management was identified by the subordinate four (4) key positions; their respective job tasks were as follows (ICMC, 1987 (b)):

> The Project Director (was) responsible to the Secretary General of ICMC. He (had) authority to make all decisions, subject to the limitations prescribed by the Secretary General. He provid(ed) direction and leadership to the entire organization, both in instructional program and administrative areas; ensure(d) effective formulation of project proposals, budget submissions, and responses to instructions and

initiative from external sources; reside(d) in Manila, with operational visits to PRPC as appropriate.

The Director of Instruction report(ed) to the Project Director, assist(ed) him by providing oversight direction and management of instructional programs at the RPC; provide(d) academic leadership, support, technical assistance and guidance to instructional program officers and staff; represent(ed) the project at academic conferences and regional meetings and act(ed) as senior official in the absence of the Project Director.

The RPC Site Officer report(ed) to the Project Director; assist(ed) in the management and supervision of the operations at RPC; (had) responsibility for general services, transportation/motorpool, civil works, building maintenance, the technical department, management of the day to day operations at RPC; and through analysis, planning and overview, assure(d) that the instructional programs receive(d) the operational support they require(d).

The Academic Officer report(ed) to the Director of Instruction; assist(ed) the Director of Instruction, acting as officer-in-charge in his absence: serve(d) as liaison between the instructional departments, personnel and registration for the overseeing of staffing requirements, and provide(d) academic support and technical assistance to instructional programs.

The Personal Officer report(ed) to the Project Director (by) initiat(ing), implement(ing) and evaluat(ing) personnel policies and services to ensure effective management.

1980 - 1984: The focus of the first administration was primarily the physical construction of the PRPC/ICMC campsite. This was no small task and could not be done without the keen ability to effectively handle the "politics" in the Filipino setting, owing to that fact that Ferdinand E. Marcos was in power (Bonner, 1987; Karnow, 1989) and his wife was the Minister of Human Settlements under which the PRPC came.[16] The accomplishments of this administration was the construction of the first two-story structure, the Instructional Media Studio, and the second to have air-conditioning, next to the PRPC hospital. This was no small feat; the idea of a two-story structure did not initially sit well with the administrator of PRPC who was a military general and opposed the obstruction of his view from his office of the picturesque mountainside. ICMC diplomacy paid off with all the site construction and development taking place during this period. The organizational energy and focus of this administration was spent on building a refugee came from scratch.

Organizational management from the staffing end was not a cause for serious concern because the project operation was small and slowly building. One of the strongest points of this administration was its communication style and process. The fact that PRPC/ICMC did not have a telephone system at that time (not until 1985) might have helped communication in that atmosphere to be personal and friendly, inspite of the fact that it seemed difficult for a Westerner to think of a bureaucracy without a telephone. In a dramatic sort of way and as the early ICMC pioneers liked to tell it, "in those days," refugee education was something novel and exciting. There was not a lot of instructional materials around on how to teach refugees because it was still in the process of being written. Teachers did not have to contend with lofty educational theories (Friere, 1983) because few seemed sure how to modify them for a refugee educational setting. There was then no training system, so the teachers taught their students in the best way they could, who in turn seemed to sense the teachers, genuineness as they appeared to have learned as well. Because the general living condition at the camp was inadequate, staff mostly had to make due with what was available. There existed little room or felt need for formality; the staff interpreted the management's style as informal and easy-going.

---

16 The Philippine Refugee Processing Center (PRPC) was a "processing center" funded by the UNHCR that gave accommodation for refugees guaranteed resettlement in other countries, primarily the U.S. The Government of the Philippines administered the Center under contract to the UNHCR. (Navarez, 1989).

One complaint however against this administration was that the style of management was more Filipino in nature (Andres, 1981; 1985); many projects were started, but few were finished. Resources and materials were mismanaged[17] with seemingly little regard for maximum use of limited resources. Towards the latter part of this administration, there was much criticism by supervisors and teachers that ICMC was negligent in following proper health and environmental codes by allowing staff dormitories, less to mention refugee billets (Podlaski, 1989) to be constructed with asbestos building materials (Marshall and Tollefson, 1989; Tollefson, 1989 (a)); asbestos being a potential cancerous agent (Herbert, 1989; Hooper, 1990: "Limited Use of Asbestos Urged," 1989). This came to be the breach in what had been generally viewed as a positive relationship between senior staff and the rank and file. The administration that followed was to inherit this unresolved issue.

The new Project Director (1984 - 1985) initially put the asbestos issue on hold, long enough to introduce the plan for instructional reorganization. Although the Project Director was a known scholar and administrator, the staff generally regarded his approach in dealing with subordinates as too heavy-handed for their liking. However, what really dampened the enthusiasm of the staff was the perception that the management had included in its operational style, "favoritism." If it liked you, you could expect to receive fair treatment, and if it did not, one needed not expect to have the benefit of being heard. Inasmuch as the Project Director had difficulty in winning staff-wide support and respect, forward movement was possible, largely because he had two senior associates that were themselves respected and liked by the staff. This administration was credited for being the architect of the cultural orientation program "New Directions," the conceptual learning model used for teaching Indochinese refugees (Redding, 1985).

Whether or not, it was true that this administration practiced staff intimidation (Tollefson, 1989 (a)), it was perceived that it did. This initially came about as a result of the administration developing and putting in place what was referred to as the Guide for Instructional Supervision and Evaluation (ICMC, 1986c) which was implemented in 1985. The significance of this document was that for the first time a "formal" process for teacher/supervisor remediation was outlined.

17 ??? that corruption was the hallmark of the Marcos era??? the general and other top military personnel??? placed there by Marcos.

As far as how the management saw it, it was intended as a tool to better identify teachers/supervisors needing professional remediation training to improve the quality of their work (Acheson and Gail, 1980). The remediation process which was under the supervision of the Program Officer entailed a written explanation of what the teacher of supervisor's deficient skill areas were and a proposed plan for improvement within a specified time limit (ICMC, 1986a). If the staff person had met the stated goals of remediation, he would be restored to a regular staff status; if not, he would be asked to resign. However, well-intended the rationale given by the management, it did little to foster a positive working relationship between teachers and supervisors. In fact, this created a strain on the teacher/supervisor's daily working relationship (ICMC, 1987 (d); White, 1988) because the supervisors were viewed as being in concert with the management's schemes. The fact that supervisors were also possible candidates for professional remediation, did not seem to fully register with teachers.

The asbestos issue reared its head once again and the administration saw that it had to do something. The number of concerned staff had grown. The management let it be known that those staff pushing the issue of asbestos were "troublemakers" (Tollefson, 1989 (a)). The administration finally tried to put the issue to rest once and for all by having a team of researchers from the Occupational Safety and Health Administration (OSHA) come to the PRPC to conduct an environmental impact study. Once this was done, the administration reported that the level of asbestos fibers in the air in the dormitories was not at or near the unacceptable level and there was no danger to anyone's health (Herbert, 1989; Hooper, 1990).

Shortly thereafter, the management even went one step further by making known a new policy that no asbestos materials would be used by ICMC in future construction projects. Existing structures (with the exception of refugee billets) using this material would as well be refurbished with other building materials.[18] Although this announcement was considered positive; nevertheless, it raised another problem: how the existing asbestos would be disposed of. This concern for a clear management statement stemmed from the "mad rush" of residents from Morong and nearby villages were making to the camp

18 In 1986, during the process when ICMC began replacing the asbestos roofs of the buildings, the Filipino workers were not provided the necessary protective clothing nor were they required to wear protective masks (Harrison, 1987 (b); Tollefson, 1989 (a)).

to get their share of asbestos building materials. Some of it had even found its way to the Morong high school (Tollefson, 1989 (a)). It was finally the decision of the management that the asbestos be removed from the area and properly disposed.

Under this administration, the staff seemed to have a growing sense of impending danger to their physical well-being. The asbestos issue was one. The second, came as the first nuclear power plant in the Philippines (Zich, 1986) located approximately twenty minutes by vehicle from the camp. The general sentiment among staff was the PRPC/ICMC community needed to be educated about living in the nuclear age in the Philippines. More pressing was the question: What contingency plans had ICMC made in the case of a nuclear mishap? The administration was tight-lipped about this and would not respond other than to say, "ICMC did have an emergency evacuation plan." The plan was simple: that in the event of a nuclear mishap, all seventeen thousand refugees and some three thousand ICMC/PRPC staff and their families were to run like hell over the big mountain due east of the camp to the South China Sea. What was supposed to happen when and if people got there was anyone's guess. The ouster of Ferdinand E. Marcos from public office on February 26, 1986 (Karnow, 1989) brought this issue to a close, the nuclear plant project was discontinued (Zich, 1986).

1985 - 1987: In April of 1985, the third administration took charge, and in the early days it was plain to see that much of the senior management's energy was devoted to how to get a handle on a project that had grown by leaps and bounds. Apart from overseeing the physical expansion of the campsite was the addition of approximately thirty new building structures within two years. This administration also put a considerable amount of energy into managing the instructional end of the project with the ambition of making the Cultural Orientation (CO) Program as viable as its English-as-a-Second Language (ESL) counterpart.

This administration, unlike the previous ones, had come to find itself faced with one of the most pressing social questions of our time: Equal Employment Opportunity (U.S. Department of Labor, 1988). The question before ICMC was whether it could afford to forgo the search for American minority-of-color representation in the CO program, if it was to effectively convey what it meant to be an American? Was it possible to uphold the idea of equal opportunity employment for all at ICMC, but do nothing to utilize qualified minority staff beyond entry level professional positions? It appeared that because of the nature of the question and the ramifications involved (EEOC, 1974): that federal policy prohibited employment discrimination on the grounds of race, color, religion, sex and national origin and in order to avoid public embarrassment, ICMC had the sensibility to state a liberal view that, as a quasi-educational institution and social services international organization, it "believed" in equal opportunity. To give evidence of its practice based on its belief, it did not ask its job applicants to indicate their race or ethnicity. Therefore, it reasoned it could not be suggested that it discriminated in its hiring practices. And yet, it claimed that it was not possible to effectively engage in "credible" American cultural orientation training of SEA refugees without "adequate" American minority representation. In an open forum in 1987, the management claimed to take the matter in hand by making an effort to identify qualified minority-of-color candidates.

It is important for the reader to understand that ICMC/ Philippines was basically an American-run project (Passage: A Journal of Refugee Education, 1987; Marshall and Tollefson, 1987; Podlaski, 1989; Ranard, 1990). Its senior staff organizational structure was composed of Americans with the exception of one foreign expatriate from New Zealand and the personnel manager, Filipino. The administration followed ICMC Geneva policy and conformed to U.S. Department of State (DOS) mandate (ICMC, 1984 (a); Tollefson, 1989 (a)). ICMC maintained a sub-office in Washington, D.C. and recruited Americans and other foreign nationals for ICMC/Philippines.

1988 - 1992: On January 1, 1988, the former Deputy Director for Operations was appointed to the post of Project Director. His selection, which required "approval" from the Secretary General of ICMC/Geneva and the DOS Bureau for Refugee Programs, seemed to bare out the thinking that they were particularly interested in getting someone already highly knowledgeable about the ICMC organization. The fact that the former Deputy Director had been with ICMC/Philippines since 1985 and knew the organization better than most, was just as important as the fact that before his posting in the Philippines, from 1982 to 1984, he served as Project Director for the ICMC/Sudan ESL/CO Project (Kristofik and Cook, 1985).

This project director inherited a house on fire and was faced with the pressing question of where to begin to try to put the fire out. To begin with, as a senior ICMC official, he was one of the least liked by the staff. Whether the basis for the perception was valid or not, he purportedly edified the legendary character of the "Ugly American." Before him loomed one of the most serious problems ICMC ever had to face: recruitment for minority-of-color candidates and upward job mobility for this group (Watts, 1987), which had taken on political (Harrison, 1987) and legal (Blassingame, 1990) ramifications. The only question left to be answered by the Project Director was whether ICMC would stop giving staff "lip service"[19] about this situation or would it take concrete action.

The Saltzman and Kern and White Consultancy Reports for 1987 and 1988, respectively, confirmed what most staff had already suspected (ICMC, 1986b; 1987 (d)); that the training system was weak, ineffectual and had little or no immediate impact on the quality of instructional services provided to refugees. The question of department reorganization seemed legitimate enough; inasmuch as, the decision rested on the project director himself (<u>NTL Institute</u>, 1984 (a)). To a good number of staff, it seemed that the ICMC Pro-Teachers Union (though not "officially" chartered with the Philippine Department of Labor) was there to stay, and at the very least, indicated to senior management the need of two-way communication (Wedersphan, 1987; White, 1988). It posed a potential danger to create political problems for ICMC that the Project Director had to decide how best a union and ICMC could co-exist in relative peace.

Another important reality was the 1988 - 1989 budget-cut to ICMC by DOS (Ranard, 1990). This made it clear that from 1988 - 1990, the main skills required of the chief executive would be to effectively tackle the situation (<u>American Management Association</u>, 1987; McCormick and Powell, 1988) and reduce the work force in the right places, build staff moral during a difficult period the organization was facing and to maintain labor stability.

The ICMC Open Forum (April, 1988) gave additional insight on what future ICMC might have after 1990. A DOS official stated: ". . . after that time DOS expect(ed) to be looking at phasing out Phanat and consolidating the training cooperation, depending on two

19 Lip service is the mouthing of insincere statements. It's telling other people what they want to hear (<u>Boardroom Classics</u>, 1989).

considerations: budget and labor stability." There was not much the Project Director could do with respect to budget cuts; however, labor stability was threatened by the ICMC Pro-teachers union (Kampo, 1988).

This administration, unlike the previous one, practiced a "low visibility" profile. One of the observations staff made was that rarely did one get to see senior management, except for their company vehicles parked almost daily in the executive parking lot. Because the Project Director was not generally liked by the staff, his absence from the camp was regarded as a blessing. No one appeared seriously concerned that at that point in time, senior staff held leadership positions in name only. The staff had given up hope of the organization finding a good executive that could "inspire" people when it gave this position to the current project director.

In March of 1987, the Director of Training for the Bureau of Refugee Programs, came to ICMC[20] as the guest at the Open Forum Management Meeting, which was held to allow ICMC staff and management to present concerns and issues. On this occasion, the Director took the opportunity to point out the separation of ICMC and DOS/Bureau for Refugee Programs with regard to the autonomy of both agencies (Tollefson, 1989 (a)). The Director stated before an audience of approximately one hundred and fifty ICMC staff, mostly instructional supervisors and teachers, that DOS had contracted ICMC to be an implementing agency for refugee training and that was where the line of cooperation by (Appendix B) Moreover, the Director wished to clear up any possible doubt that her office had authority or interest in "interfering" in the internal policies of ICMC, as such action would be overstepping its bounds. She emphasized that the concerns of one party should be raised to the other because this was seen as keeping with the spirit of openness and cooperation. This statement was, however, contrary to the actual practice (U.S. Agency for International Development, 1994).

Human behavior is such that rarely does one bite the hand that feeds it; ICMC in its relationship with DOS was no different (Tollefson, 1989 (a)). The Director failed to remember that in March, ICMC/Philippines had posted a position opening for a Program Officer for the Cultural Orientation (CO) Program advertised

20 Once a year the Director of Training, Bureau for Refugee Programs. U.S. Department of State, conducted a field visit to ICMC/Philippines.

nationally and internationally. This position would have likely gone to the Acting Program Officer of the CO program, a Filipino that had applied for the post. The Acting Program Officer reportedly had the support and backing of senior management. A few days before the application deadline, ICMC was notified by DOS (Appendix E) that one requirement it was adding for the position was that the candidates for consideration for the post had to possess [stateside] resettlement experience. The situation was such that led the Project Director to immediately apply "damage control," however, appropriately disguised (Appendix E). The position finally went to an American, who was the person that DOS had in mind.

Usually, DOS briefings to ICMC/Philippines staff were formal and diplomatic much inspite of the stated "informality" it claimed to prefer. In March of 1987 at an Open Forum Management Meeting, the writer took the liberty to ask about the question of Affirmative Action (EEOC, 1974).

> Since the overseas resettlement agencies operating in SEA also comprise American-based agencies, like the Experiment in International Living, World Education, and World Relief receive project funding from DOS; doesn't the fact that they are U.S. incorporated, that in order to receive funding and be looked on favorably by DOS, they either submit an Affirmative Action plan with the project proposal or subscribe to the Title VII of the Civil Rights Act of 1964?

The reply from the Director of Training, Bureau of Refugee Programs was that the question was an ICMC/Philippines matter; furthermore, DOS wielded "no power" that could be used to influence ICMC policy. It was a fact that American overseas resettlement agencies had <u>less</u> minority-of-color representation on its staff than ICMC. DOS did not express intent to monitor Affirmative Action/ Equal Employment Opportunity practices of its implementing agencies using U.S. funds. Hence, it was simply logical that ICMC would be the <u>last</u> agency that would be singled out by DOS for criticism about this issue.

One illustration of ICMC racial discrimination practices was its denial of request for lateral transfer from Work Orientation (WO) program after 3 years to the Cultural Orientation (CO) program of an African-American supervisor for the reason that he lacked U.S. resettlement experience (Blassingame, 1990). Yet, without reservation, ICMC "hired" an Englishman (Anglo) who according to his own account had spent the total of four months in the U.S. as a "tourist" (much less ever having worked there). Would such an intervention in ICMC policy by DOS be viewed as an interference? Would DOS voluntarily offer a timely comment on such a situation? (Chap. X analyzes this case in detail.)

In the final analysis, the 1985 - 1987 administration did not initiate "corrective" measures to aid the refugees' or the Filipino staff's knowledge of American life from the perspective of the American minority-of-color which could have been done by altering the racial composition of its staff (Breaugh, 1992; Sargent, 1984; Watts, 1987; U.S. Department of Labor, 1988). Finally, the single most important dynamic which could have changed the nature of refugee resettlement, how it was conceived and done, and who did it was the Department of State. Without it, there would have been no ICMC/Philippines (Passage: A Journal of Refugee Education, 1987).

Organizational Communication

One of the primary indicators often used to determine the overall effectiveness of any management is to consider how well it communicates its organizational philosophy, policies, goals and objectives to its members. It has long been considered a truism that the management's ability to communicate in an appropriate fashion is critical (Drucker, 1977, Brittel and Ramsey, 1988) to being able to get the job done. Most organizations in their determination to be effective in accomplishing the task before it, use assessment instruments to find out how well the management is handling its part in the communications process. In 1987, ICMC conducted its first program-wide Communications Survey (Wederspahn, 1987) which scored moderately high: 2+ on a 5 point scale.

> More than 300 staff contributed, through the questionnaires or interviews to a survey aimed at assessing the "quality" of communication at ICMC.
>
> The results of the survey consisted of charts showing responses to the scaled items and an analysis of the 850 comments, broken down both by the specific organizational grouping respondent were referring to (a department or job level) and by category (the types of problems or issues respondent identified). Appendices included a list of 35 suggestions for action that might be taken and all of the verbatim comments.

Meanwhile, some ICMC staff were actively forming a union for the purpose of gaining better communication with management.

In any case, the survey results called attention to communications "problems" within ICMC and some of the factors:

> Problems in getting information. (Receiving vague or contradictory information; the people who should be able to provide information being unable to; lack of access to the person who can help; physical or program structure factors which impede; requests for more feedback on your performance.)
>
> Timeliness of communication. (Getting the information needed when needed; out-dated communication.)
>
> Communication systems needs. (Need to learn through official channels rather than the grapevine; avoiding channel blockages such as red tape; streamlining of the system for getting messages to and from Manila; need for a systematic way to provide bottom-up information; refinement of the way to sign up for trips or request other services.)
>
> Role definitions: whom to go to for what. (Knowing what it is each department does and the functions of each person in it; having clear idea of who should talk to whom about what, under what circumstances.)
>
> Policies and procedures. (Having a clear statement available of the organization's policies, especially in such areas as personnel; knowing standard operating procedures and having them followed consistently; having in-put in the drafting of policies which directly affect one.)
>
> Methods of communication. (This category includes comments and suggestions regarding meetings, other types of face-to-face interactions, mail and messages, phones, radio and telex, memos, other written materials like minutes and newsletters, and many

comments on the Management Forum,[21] which people like but want to see changed in format.)

Attitudes affecting communication. (Staff want management to show frankness, sincerity, honesty, openness, lack of defensiveness, interest and concern for them. Staff want other staff to treat them with courtesy, equality, without arrogance, condescension, grouchiness or "sour faces.")

This survey also provided an overview of job levels of how staff in instructional programs perceived communication operating between the different levels within the organization:

1. In looking at communication among job levels in the instructional programs, the highest level of dissatisfaction was the supervisors with senior management. One of the highest levels of satisfaction was teachers' with their supervisors.

2. The major organizational groups to receive comments regarding dissatisfaction with their communications were senior management and personnel.

21 The Management Forum (ICMC, 1988 (f)) indicated that no action by senior management was taken on the matter, even though it reiterated that it thought a change in forum format was "a good idea."

Research, Development and Planning As A Management Tool

The following five (5) years, ICMC expanded its use of computers to the point where it had its own computer center in addition to-one instructional program (Preparation for American School Systems, PASS) with computer center laboratory for students and teacher use. This enhanced the capability of ICMC to become more efficient in a wide range of areas: administration, instructional support services, scheduling and student registration. Rightly or wrongly, there existed among the 1,069 local Filipino staff (ICMC, 1987 (i)), the notion that this sophisticated gadgetry would ultimately be judged in direct relationship to how well research, development and planning activities were handled in three basic areas: 1. reduction in workforce, 2. displaced ICMC workers and re-entry into the Philippine labor market and 3. community relations.

Many Filipino staff found it hard to grasp fully what was happening in the face of ICMC downsizing activities. They were "officially" put on notice that conceivably after twenty-four (24) months they might not have a job with ICMC, some sooner than others (ICMC, 1988 (f)) because the project would be phased out. Ironically, the planned reduction of the ICMC workforce had not stopped senior management from purchasing a "new" fleet of vehicles to ride around; building a two-story administration building; much less to mention adding positions at the executive level. If anything, "objective" observation suggested, things appeared to be booming.

Meanwhile, in a country such as the Philippines that was politically unstable and in dire economic straights ("Aquinos' Rule is Imperiled As Foes Multiply And People Power Grows Frail," 1990) working in a refugee camp where things appeared to be economically booming, any reduction in the workforce of Filipinos had to be approached and handled with care. Anything short of this could bring about an adverse reaction. This was the case in 1986 when the United Nations High Commissioner for Refugees (UNHCR) unexpectedly reduced the funding level of the (PRPC) that subsequently, had no choice but to reduce the number of its staff. Some workers were issued "pink slips" and told they no longer had a job. Many of those terminated felt desperation and anger and had the sympathy and support of (former) fellow workers. Together they held a demonstration at the main entrance to PRPC. For three days it was not possible for workers to enter or leave the camp as the protesters had the entrance to the PRPC blocked. The same held true for vehicles which could not enter or leave camp. At the end of the first day, the strikers agreed to allow staff and vehicles to exit from the PRPC; however, the only people that were permitted to enter were in-bound refugees to the camp.

As one could imagine, tension was high between the demonstrators and PRPC officials. The possibility of violence erupting was real. The demonstrators seemed to be motivated by the appearance of a thriving and prospering environment and then having to reckon with the seeming contradiction that their agency funding was reduced.

ICMC and the other agencies at the PRPC took "special" note of this kind of undesirable situation, and the need to conduct the needed research, development and planning in this area (when and how some 1000 plus staff would be finally phased-out of their jobs). It was a positive sign that ICMC had shown some sensitivity to this on a basic level (Esty, 1988; NTL Institute, 1984 (a)).

Displaced Workers and Re-entry to the Philippines Labor Market

It was purported (ICMC, 1987 (i); 1988 (f)) that no one knew exactly how the project phase-out was to be conducted, only that the process would be "systematic and fair." Still, several questions remained in staff members minds whether verbally spoken or not. Some of these questions were: Would the phase-out be gradual, say fifty (50) or sixty (60) employees at a time (Esty, 1988)? Would employees seniority with the agency be a factor? Would there be some kind of out-counseling provided to departing employees? Would higher management jobs be on the cutting block at the same time as others (McCormick and Powell, 1988)? Would a ICMC Workers Union be in a position to "officially" discuss the issue of severance pay with ICMC management?

According to the American Management Association (AMA) (1987), the general trend in the reduction of the workforce or "downsizing" was less of a phenomena than a means to become more efficient and productive. As in the case of ICMC/Philippines, however, downsizing approaches and strategies were the organizational dynamics applied in the eventuality of project termination (Esty, 1988). At any rate, with the political and public relations dimensions of moving to reduce such a large and concentrated workforce, DOS had to consider a severance pay package to reasonably satisfy all parties concerned.

Facing a projected thirty-six (36) month count-down to phase-out (Marshall and Tollefson, 1989), ICMC engaged in conducting research on the projected future state of the Filipino labor market's capability to absorb 1000 plus professionals, skilled and semi-skilled workers (Gaston, 1987). The training system was charged with responsibility for further developing Filipinos in particular by offering university advanced degree studies for instructional staff members interested in professional self-development (ICMC, 1986 (c); Ranard and Pfleger, 1995). This "self-development" education program was conducted at PRPC by two Filipino institutions of higher education. Participants in this program, with approval of ICMC management, used a portion of work time to devote to academic studies. The only criticism made to management about this was that the course offerings and degree programs were limited to the field of education (ICMC, 1986 (c); White, 1988) when the Philippines was already saturated with teachers.

In 1987, a consultant was contracted by ICMC to come up with a questionnaire for teachers that would analyze their skills and how these could possibly be related to post ICMC employment. This questionnaire was dubbed as the Re-entry Packet (Gaston, 1987). In some respects, after the questionnaire was completed in the latter part of September, 1987, it raised a sense of false hope because management some months later denied that the purpose of the questionnaire was an attempt to direct staff to open job markets, they said it was for the teachers' own reference to use the information as they saw fit. Moreover, the results of the questionnaire were not tabulated and scored (ICMC, 1988 (d)). All things considered, ICMC had initiated steps to prepare staff for the eventuality of a reduction in workforce (Esty, 1988; ICMC, 1987 (b)). This activity which the rank-and-file referred to as "Life After ICMC" became one of the management objectives until the closure of the project.

In defining what made up the activities in preparing for employment after ICMC (Navarez, 1989), it became apparent that ICMC was providing an outplacement service. The term "outplacement" is "generally, any assistance in finding new employment for displaced workers . . . everything qualifies: a 10-minute meeting on the shop floor where workers are briefed on their benefits, direct individual aid and counseling, and every step between." (AMA, 1987)

As mentioned previously, ultimately, ICMC would come to be judged by its staff, in part, on the basis of how well it prepared workers to re-enter the Philippine labor market. This judgment would, no doubt, include the outplacement services which were provided to staff members, more especially, the "quality" and "quantity" of those. The more knowledge one had of how to quantify human services in this area, the more credible would be the final judgment. The beginning point for consideration would appropriately be: How to quantify a company's commitment to outplacement assistance? Three good measures existed: (1) The scope of services provided; (2) the range of workers to whom such services are offered; and (3) the cost of those services to the company. The AMA gathered data on all three measures. The first two items, scope and cost have immediate application to the ICMC situation using the data gathered by AMA.

Scope

AMA developed a checklist of 15 specific outplacement services. Each is briefly defined . . . in order of their popularity among our respondents. Exhibit 6.1 provides statistical breakdown for these options by both company size and category.

Resume Development. A resume, brief review of an individual's work and personal history, highlights the qualifications, experience, background, and accomplishments that make an employee a solid candidate for a specific job. It is a major tool in any job search, and its successful development often depends on the skills and knowledge of the counselor providing the guidance. A resume is usually necessary for an interview, and having a well-developed resume can clearly be a confidence booster to the job applicant.

Eighty-nine of the 100 firms offering assistance aided workers in resume development, making it by far the leading form of help. Every one of the 33 large companies that rendered outplacement assistance helped with resume development.

Interview Training. The interview is the arena where the applicant sells himself or herself, usually on a face-to-face basis. It is vital that the applicant appear confident and act naturally in this interface; interview training reduces anxiety and tension by preparing the applicant for the difficult questions and/or situations that may arise during the actual interview.

Seventy-two firms provided interview training as an outplacement service, including two-thirds of the small companies offering outplacement assistance. Service firms were somewhat more likely to provide such training than manufacturers.

Benefits Counseling. An explanation of the various company plans, as well as company termination policies and procedures with respect to severance dollars (the amount and how they are paid), health and life insurance, pension status, unused vacation time, sick leave, and other such benefits, can serve to reduce some of the tension and economic pressures experienced by the terminee.

Sixty firms provided benefits counseling. Again, service companies lead manufacturers in doing so; small firms were as likely as large ones to offer this service.

Skill/Interest Assessment. Assessment implies some type of formal or informal testing program, using various materials and methods. An assessment attempt to isolate and/or measure the individual's physical and/or mental proficiencies that enable him or her to perform given tasks. The same skill can be central to the execution of more than one task, thus, it is useful in variety of job functions and across occupational fields.

Interest assessment for the most part probes an individual's preferences, attitudes, and interests in different fields of work. One of the goals of assessment is to expand the career options open to the individual, who may show qualifications for occupations not previously considered. By expanding career options, assessment can build confidence and widen a worker's professional horizons.

Exhibit 6.1 Outplacement benefits checklist (percentage of firms offering these benefits as part of their outplacement support).

		Size				Category			
	All	No Answer	Large	Mid	Small	Mfg.	Service	Other	No Answer
Offered services	100	9	21	32	38	35	50	14	1
(Pct. of whole sample)	47.6%	56.3%	63.6%	53.3%	37.6%	44.3%	45.9%	66.7%	100.0%
Benefits counseling	60	6	14	16	24	18	33	9	0
	60.0%	66.7%	66.7%	50.0%	63.2%	51.4%	66.0%	64.3%	0.0%
Skill/Interest assessment	58	5	13	18	22	21	28	8	1
	58.0%	55.6%	61.9%	56.3%	57.9%	60.0%	56.0%	57.1%	100.0%
Resume development	89	8	21	27	34	31	43	14	1
	89.0%	88.9%	100.0%	84.4%	89.5%	88.6%	86.0%	100.0%	100.0%
Mailings	46	4	11	18	13	17	22	6	1
	46.0%	44.4%	52.4%	56.3%	34.2%	48.6%	44.0%	42.9%	100.0%
Interview training	72	5	17	25	25	23	37	11	1

	72.0%	55.6%	81.0%	78.1%	65.8%	65.7%	74.0%	73.6%	100.0%
Labor/Job market info	56	6	11	18	21	23	24	8	1
	56.0%	66.7%	52.4%	56.3%	55.3%	65.7%	48.0%	57.1%	100.0%
Out-of-area search	26	4	9	8	5	8	13	5	0
	26.0%	44.4%	42.9%	25.0%	13.2%	22.9%	26.0%	35.7%	0.0%
Follow-up services	41	4	10	12	15	16	18	6	1
	41.0%	44.4%	47.6%	37.5%	39.5%	45.7%	36.0%	42.9%	100.0%
Career resource center	27	3	8	10	6	7	16	4	0
	27.0%	33.3%	38.1%	31.3%	15.8%	20.0%	32.0%	28.6%	0.0%
Peer support groups	19	1	6	3	9	4	11	4	0
	19.0%	11.1%	28.6%	9.4%	23.7%	11.4%	22.0%	28.6%	0.0%
Remediation/ education	3	1	1	0	1	1	1	1	0
	3.0%	11.1%	4.8%	0.0%	2.6%	2.9%	2.0%	7.1%	0.0%
GED prep	2	1	1	0	0	0	1	1	0
	2.0%	11.1%	4.8%	0.0%	0.0%	0.0%	2.0%	7.1%	0.0%
On-site unemployment	6	1	2	1	2	2	4	0	0
	6.0%	11.1%	9.5%	3.1%	5.3%	5.7%	8.0%	0.0%	0.0%
Counseling-finance	25	3	9	6	8	8	12	5	0
	25.0%	33.3%	42.9%	15.6%	21.1%	22.9%	24.0%	35.7%	0.0%
Counseling-family	22	3	9	3	7	6	12	3	1
	22.0%	33.3%	42.9%	9.4%	18.4%	17.1%	24.0%	21.4%	100.0%

Reprinted by permission of the publisher, from Responsible Reduction In Force: An American Management Association Research Report On Downsizing and Outplacement, copyright 1987 pp. 61-64. New York: American Management Association. (All rights reserved.)

Fifty-eight companies performed skill/interest assessments for terminated workers. In each of the sample's subsets — small, medium, or large firms; manufacturers, service providers, or others — more than half the respondents offering any outplacement services provided assessment.

Job Market Information. Services that include information on the current labor market serve to focus job search efforts more precisely on those areas with the greatest opportunity of employment for the terminee. While the data in many cases may be somewhat sketchy, it nevertheless helps to eliminate some of the wasted time and effort that goes into a job search.

Job-seekers who are armed with information about where and what jobs are available, appropriate companies to target, and potential salary levels have a leg up in the job-seeking campaign.

Fifty-six companies gathered job market information to share with terminated employees. Two-thirds of the manufacturers among them did so, compared with less than half the service companies.

Out-of-Area Job Searches,[22] a separate item on the AMA checklist, helped to broaden the options available to terminated workers, especially at the executive level. Twenty-six forms included out-of-area information as part of their assistance efforts, with large companies (43 percent) far more likely to look beyond the local horizon than small ones (13 percent).

Mailings. Mail campaigns broadcast the availability of terminated workers. While letters from individuals seeking employment are often filed away as soon as they are received, a letter from an employer asking consideration for a terminated worker may have a special impact. Letters are not considered a particularly fruitful method of finding employment, but on occasion they will lead to interviews and subsequent job offers.

Forty-six firms performed mailings on behalf of terminated workers. Half the large and mid-sized companies did so, compared with just a third of the small ones.

Follow-up Services. The question has more to do with the period in which assistance is provided than with the specific services the employer performs. Follow-up services display a long-term commitment to terminated workers and, like other forms of assistance, build good moral among "survivors" who remain with the company.

Forty-one firms provided follow-up services of some type, with large companies (48 percent) leading the mid-sized (38 percent) and small (40 percent) firms. At this point in the checklist, a statistical note is necessary. As the number of companies in the sample providing

22 An ESL staff member was chosen to represent ICMC/Philippines at the Japan Association of Language Teachers (JALT) Conference in Japan. On her return, she presented a paper reporting possibilities for future employment of ICMC staff as English teachers in Japan (ICMC, 1988b).

any single service diminishes, differences by corporate size or business category have less statistical import. Obviously, a small sample is not as statistically accurate as a large one, and we are now dealing with ever-smaller subsets within the 100 companies that offer some form of outplacement assistance: small, mid-sized, and large firms, manufacturers, service providers, and "others," which include diversified conglomerates. Fewer than 30 percent of the 100 firms under current study provide any of the checklist items that follow, and the reader should continue with that in mind.

Career Resource Center. Such a center opens up a variety of services for certain levels of employees who have been terminated. These services can include physical space, furniture and equipment, office supplies, and secretariat support, as well as research references, job postings, and other employment information.

A career resource center can fulfill a number of needs during the search process, ranging from an improved capability to conduct actual day-to-day activities to the psychological support needed by the job-seeker to complete the search successfully.

Service companies (32 percent) proved more likely to provide this sort of support than manufacturers, and large (38 percent) and mid-size (31 percent) forms were far more engaged in such support than small ones (16 percent).

Counseling on Personal Finance. A review of the terminated employee's personal finances may focus on both current status and future prospects. The service enables the individual to select from among the different career options available and choose the course of action that is best suited to his or her needs. For example, counselors can supply some of the necessary data needed to make a decision as to whether the person can afford to undertake an entrepreneurial venture or commission-type work, rather than search for a salaried position.

Counseling on family matters helps terminated employees to deal better with family problems during the stressful period that follow notice of termination. A concomitant of employee assistance programs for all employees, family counseling can better arm the worker and his or her family to deal with the straitened circumstances that often accompany unemployment and the search for a new job.

Peer Support Groups. "You are not Alone" is an important message for terminated employees, who may find that a problem shared is more easily borne. Many companies offer one-time "gripe sessions," where terminated workers can air their anger and grievances; fewer encourage ongoing peer support, which may well prove far more helpful, boosting morale and confidence during the job search and allowing information to be shared.

Nineteen firms organized peer support groups, with services companies (22 percent) twice as likely to do so as manufacturers (11 percent).

On-Site Unemployment Setup. Special arrangements with state, city or local entitles may allow workers to register with government employments bureaus at the work site. Such as effort gives corporate concern a physical form, and eases the way for employees who otherwise would suffer through long lines and impersonal processing.

Six companies — four service providers, two manufacturers — arranged on-site unemployment desks with government officials.

Remediation and Basic Education. This, together with GED (high-school equivalency) Exam Preparation, offers help to those who may be most in need. Illiteracy in the workplace is an on-going problem, and not only at the lower levels. According to a 1985 U.S. Training Industry survey, approximately 25 percent of the 2,600 firms polled were offering programs in "basic and remedial education," up from 18 percent in 1984.

Summary. An overview of the statistical findings offers few surprises. In most cases, large companies prove more likely to provide a particular service than mid-sized or small ones, but the gap is not so large as might be expected. In one regard — providing job market information — small companies actually lead large and mid-size firms. The greatest gaps exist where physical and financial resources are most at issue: Large firms are twice as likely to provide individual financial or family counseling, and 38 percent of them find space for a career resource center, compared with 16 percent of small companies. Service firms are somewhat more likely to provide job information and physical support to terminated employees. But to say that large firms evince greater concern for displaced workers than smaller ones is far from the mark.

As of April 1989, ICMC was engaged in these areas of outplacement benefits counseling, skills interest assessment, job market information, graduate school sponsorship (not previously listed) and resume development shown in illustration.

ICMC showed initial weakness in the area of follow-up, one of the most important functions (Boardroom Classics, 1989, Tollefson, 1989 (a)), which otherwise, improved with better logistical planning and coordination. With the exception of Peer Support Groups, ICMC to some extent had moved into all of the areas mentioned by AMA Cost.

The cost of offering outplacement services depends to a great extent on who takes on the assignment. In roughly equal degree, respondents counted on in-house staff (34 percent), a contracted agency (36 percent), or the two acting in combination (29 percent). See Exhibit 6.3.

Source: Gecko (June, 1988).

Small companies were far more likely to take a "do-it-yourself" approach: 47 percent of the small firms offering out placement services performed the tasks entirely in-house, compared with 31 percent of the mid-sized firms and just 10 percent of the large ones. Executive outplacement firms have long targeted the Fortune 1000 as clients, their future growth depends on moving beyond that favored list, for the giant companies have made their choices. Four in 10 put an outside agency in charge of outplacement, and 5 in 10 worked in combination with a contracted service.

The choice of provider makes a difference in costs, according to respondents that gave us figures. Again, averages (or means) are less important here than modes, the most frequently given responses, or medians, making the midway points at which as many respondents reported a higher figure as a lower one. Exhibit 6.4, also gives the highest per-person cost reported, and the lowest.

Exhibit 6.4.	Outplacement Services — per-person costs provided by		
Mean	In-house Staff	Outside Organization	Combined
Mean	$840	$1,634	$3,912
Median	310	306	1,950
Mode	*240	1,000	*1,500
	*350		*6,000
High	5,100	12,500	17,000
Low	30	120	150

* — Two modes reported

Source: AMA. 1987.

With variations so large, further explanation is necessary. The range of services provided is the greatest factor impacting costs: naturally, the more a company seeks to do for its terminated workers, the higher its expenses.

A review of the ICMC/DOS literature and documents show that outplacement activity became the responsibility of the Personnel Department. Human Resources Division and the Training System (ICMC, 1986 (c): White, 1988).

Exhibit 6.3, can be considered being representative by percentage breakdown of how the task was broken down and parceled out to respective in-house departments and outside agencies, or a combination of the two. In the case of ICMC, it did not indicate the participation of DOS as its co-partner by virtue of their Cooperative Agreement.

ICMC via the DOS cooperative agreement still had an on-going need to bring in "outside" resources, which were not necessarily at the agency level (Harmon, 1985). Frequently, ICMC went through DOS to identify and contract individuals whose expertise ICMC needed to advance its outplacement activities. Together ICMC/DOS made a regular practice of "combining" in-house staff and outside agency/individual expertise in an effort to bring the appropriate resources to bare on the immediate task.

Community Relations

ICMC had difficulty being able to get its Community Relations Program off the ground. This referred to its relationship with the town of Morong seven (7) kilometers from PRPC. One problem was that the management was not clear on the nature of relationship it wished to cultivate Since most of the residents of Morong had a definite idea about the relationship they wanted with ICMC: "to be given a job," it found itself under pressure to make good on its stated intent to foster community involvement and enrichment. In principle, the project director passed a memo that a percentage of jobs would go to Morong residents (Cook, 1988). It sounded promising, but needed to be taken with a grain of salt by professionals or college graduates who wished to work for ICMC. Most of the positions management had in mind was for manual laborers.

A considerable part of the difficulty had to do with the fact that ICMC was a large organization based in a fishing village, where many of its residents had little comprehension of a modern day organization functioning. Naturally, people tended to project to ICMC and others in their surroundings how they thought it should function and conduct itself in their community. Because of this, it was understandable, why ICMC chose in actual practice of community relations to assume the posture of the "sleeping giant," a fitting description of how ICMC coped with its insecurity, ambivalence and dilemma with the Morong community. On one hand, ICMC stated its desire to become involved in community development but in the process was aware that there existed a different reality which it was hard pressed to understand and deal with. One good walk through Morong was enough to convince anyone of the many pressing needs it had. The problem facing ICMC was how to go about becoming a "partner" in community development without having to take a serious setback should it had made a wrong move. All evidence seemed to point to ICMC taking the position: that it had too much at stake and too much to lose.

It was unfortunate that the situation had been viewed in these terms because of the sheer amount of material and human resources that ICMC possessed,[23] for example, the pens, paper and other school materials that found its way into countless homes in Morong. With all due fairness to ICMC, the "risks" involved were real. There were at least two political incidents which could have been flashpoints, as a result of ICMC wider community involvement. Leftist political organizations in the Philippines as the Communist Party of the Philippines (CCP) and New People's Army (NPA) (Chapman, 1987) were actively operating in the Bataan, province (Karnow, 1989) that quite possibly could have taken issue with the "Americans," taking a hand in the needs of the Filipino community. ICMC had been able to avoid this because it had remained an island unto itself. Reality notwithstanding, it was also true that ICMC had not approached this obstacle with any view to developing possible alternatives and solutions to the problem.

---

23 In 1994, one year before its close, ICMC/ Philippines sought "approval" from DOS to dispose of its property (ICMC, 1994). In the "Property Disposition Summary" (Appendix B) it proposed allocating the province of Bataan assets i.e., educational materials and equipment valued at $90,278.

Personnel Administration of ICMC Multi-National Staff: How It Was Done

Noted in the Wederspahn, 1987 Communications Survey that the personnel department was regarded by most, irrespective of hiring category, to be one of the most complicated systems to negotiate when the need arose.

From the inception of ICMC/Philippines to its closure, there existed a separate personnel policy manual for international and local hires.[24] International hire staff were Americans and other foreign expatriates recruited and/or processed directly by ICMC/Washington. This nomenclature could be further used to determine what salary the person was paid and in what currency. International hires were remunerated for their work in ("tax free") U.S. dollars. Filipino local hires were paid in their currency (peso). Unlike the Americans, Filipinos were required to pay taxes and other customary salary deductions. The Filipino staff members having queries of a personnel nature went to the personnel department and discussed them with the appropriate representative. The local hire section of the personnel department was managed by Filipino staff. The international hire staff would bring their concerns to the international hire Personnel Coordinator (ICMC, 1987 (b)). This person was a foreign expatriate. The human dynamic involved here seemed to bare out that in the matter of "taking care of business," it was practice to help things along by seeing to it that staff had the benefit of talking in the same language.

24 The only identical policy to be found in the international and local hire policy manual was the employee codified penalties and professional code of ethnics.

In the last decade, one of the necessary roles of the personnel department in many organizations has been to tackle the social issue of equality in the development of human resources. It is a concept that fosters equality for anybody not to be denied opportunities and protection from unfair and/or illegal forms of discrimination. In the case of ICMC, the political and social ramifications of the DOS/ICMC Cooperative Agreement had fallen in the lap of the personnel department to clarify to Filipino nationals why the difference in payscale and benefits between local and international hire staff; the most common example cited (White, 1988) was the Filipino and American supervisors having the same job responsibilities but different pay and benefits.

An effective personnel department that has the distinction of being looked on favorably is adept at dealing with the issues which individuals or groups bring for clarification and resolution, even in instances beyond its ability to satisfy the staff to the desired point of satisfaction. Social psychology posits that to have a basic understanding of what makes people tick, can be of great value to people whose job it is to also deal with understanding other people they serve. Human relations is the key to a good personnel operation but as in cases where policies and regulations that are not necessarily popular, must be followed. An example of this situation was the concern Filipino local hire staff of possibly being "exploited" by ICMC because of the difference in the payscale and pay currency existing between international and local hire staff. Equal pay for equal work was their rallying motto. The decision in reality did not rest with the personnel department. However, resentment and frustration was targeted to it.

An analysis of the Filipino staff dissatisfaction with ICMC in general, and salary remuneration in particular seemed to reflect the labor unrest of the socio-political milieu in Philippine society ("Strikes Vs. Industrial Peace," 1988). When ICMC went on record that it expected to terminate project operations in the not-too-distant future and would "officially" begin reducing its workforce by 1990 (ICMC, 1988 (f)), the local staff took this as being the worst eventuality that could be imagined (White, 1988). Thus, their rationale for group action was that their financial situation would not be as concerning if they were paid in U.S. dollars, just like the international-hires. Since this was not going to materialize, fuel was added to the fire by accusations that they were "exploited" ("A Look at the Union Core Group," 1988).

The unique set of circumstance involved in ICMC personnel management can be viewed from a wider framework of facts customary in the Philippine setting. Multi-national and international organizations pay their local employees in the local currency[25] (Denton and Villena-Denton, 1986) and have "long been regarded" as a place of work where one could hardly expect to earn the same salary from a Filipino company. Multi-national forms in the Philippines have a better record of treating their employees fairly.

ICMC local-hire employees payscale was purported by the personnel department to be on parity with local-hire staff of the American Embassy in Manila. It was also in step with salary increments, cost of living allowance and other related benefits the U.S. Embassy provides its Filipino employees.

The third largest employer to the Philippine government was the U.S. government (Zich, 1986), principally employing skilled Filipino manpower at the military bases (Clark Air Force Base and Subic Naval Base). These employees just like the U.S. Embassy personnel were paid in the local currency and by all accounts were paid well (Shenson, 1991). These two military installations had experienced their share of labor disputes centering around the issue of pay increases. In one such case, a Filipino worker hired as a "temporary worker" during a union strike was beaten and killed before he could reach the main entrance to the base. However, these disputes were not regular, and the general impression was that they were given a fair deal.

What must also not be overlooked during the U.S. and Philippine governments negotiation over the bases' was the demand of Filipino workers for <u>more</u> money ("Subic Base Facility Hit By Strike," 1988). The very idea that a stable and reliable employer could one day leave[26] seemed to be enough for employees to feel that before the gravy train picked up and left town for good, "I'll be dam if I'm not going to get my full."

This seemed to be the main reason why local-hire ICMC staff would go to the personnel department and cry bloody murder in preparation for "Life After ICMC" (Navarez, 1989).

---

25 The writer devoted considerable time and energy to this question: "Who sets the policy regarding what currency a Filipino worker may be paid in?" It is his understanding that the Ministry of Labor does not allow for a "resident" Filipino to be remunerated in another currency other than pesos.

26 The volcano eruption of Mt. Pinatubo in June 1991 forced the U.S. military to abandon Clark Air Base ("Aquino's Rule is Imperiled As Foes Multiply and People Power Grows Frail," 1991; "Epitaph: A Base Named Clark," 1991).

Program Management Plan

Each year, ICMC/Philippines developed and submitted to DOS a Program Management Plan (PMP). This plan was a "blueprint" of how program objectives with respect to the DOS/ICMC Cooperative Agreement would be met. Apart from this, important management tool, the PMP was one of the few ICMC "official" documents that made clear the management's belief that there existed a relationship between the success of the project and having within the agency international hire i.e., "American" staff. It was thought that the international hire factor was a variable which made the project effective in relation to the positions they occupied and the general number and/or percentages they made up within the organization:

> The effectiveness of the program operation and the quality of the results the program achieves [depend] . . . on the caliber of the international staff, who hold key positions in the organization. We will be striving to improve ICMC recruitment efforts, and to obtain the best qualified candidates for positions from Instructional Supervisor through Program Officer.
>
> These objectives are [specific and measurable] (ICMC, 1987 (b)).

However, White (1988) introduced the idea of changing the supervisory job description in order to be able to "measure" the [productive and qualitative] input of international hire supervisors into the program. As it stood, Filipino and international hire supervisors had the same job description.[27] Based on this, it was empirically difficult if not impossible to measure the qualitative worth, or the extra special that international hires brought with them into the program which the Filipino supervisors did not. Another parallel argument advanced was the generic job description for both Filipino and international-hire supervisors that if the two produced measurable qualitative work at the same level, "there was no point in recruiting international-hire from the U.S." (Hunter, 1987), since qualified Filipinos could be recruited for supervisory positions.

Reports coming from senior management regarding the 1988 PMP, informed staff that 1988 was designated as the year the project would initiate, as part of the PMP, a program- wide downsizing scheme (Esty, 1988; AMA, 1987), with the realization that this could well mean not only reducing the workforce, but trying to produce a better quality of human service.

27 In December 1990, the job description for international hire "Instructional Supervisor" was changed to "International Resource Specialist," while the title job title of Instructional Supervisor remained for Filipinos.

Cooperative Agreement

The Cooperative Agreement between ICMC/Philippines and U.S. Department of State (DOS) had existed since 1980, the purpose outlined fully in Article I (Appendix B) which stated in part:

> WHEREAS, the Bureau is conduting a program as authorized under the applicable provisions of the Migration and Refugee Assistance Act of 1962, as amended; and
>
> WHEREAS, the Bureau deems it appropriate to seek ICMC's assistance in furtherance of the purpose of this program;
>
> WHEREAS, ICMC has expressed its willingness to continue implementing the Program and has submitted a Management Plan . . .

Government provision by means of a cooperative agreement to conduct foreign policy in order to further its own interest is a complex set of arrangements, procedures and processes. This is due to working thru a second or even third party to implement a plan. It is generally believed that operational guidelines and procedures for carrying out the mandate of the principal agent is sufficient to bring about the desired goal. In this case, DOS delegated monitoring and accountability functions to a specific office or department that usually had the authority to recommend, suspend or terminate the agreement in the instance where it was not being executed to the satisfaction of the government or was no longer in its interest.

The Bureau for Refugee Programs directed the ICMC program without any regular presence at PRPC, except for a week to ten days visit once or twice a year of its Director and Assistant Director of the Office of Training. These visits were based on the precept that it was not possible to run a project like this effectively from behind a desk in Washington. If it were possible for one or two visits a year to be beneficial, it was significantly reduced because ICMC played host to these "V.I.P.'s" by bringing fanfare and ceremony to these so-called "working visits." By-and-large, these visits by the Director of Training were given to budget aspects of the agreement more than anything else. In any case, they were not in the setting long enough to have a chance to take off their rose-colored glasses.

DOS knew that it required several different key operational elements on its part to oversee this particular of agreement. For this reason, the Bureau for Refugee Programs had parceled out the responsibility and monitoring functions of the agreement to various entities within the Department from Washington, D.C. to the American Embassies in Manila and Thailand. What follows is an outline of what offices and related personnel and organizational structures were necessary and responsible for certain aspects of the cooperative agreement.

Description of Sectors, Responsibility and Components of Assistance

1. Bureau for Refugee Programs, Office of Training (Location Washington, D.C.) provided overall policy guidance and program direction; reviewed and commented on proposed budget and changes or revisions in terms of agreements; approved any changes in program specifications or design, subject to the availability of funds; and negotiated with the government of the Philippines, through the Refugee Coordinator, for overall permission to conduct this program in the camp.
2. Refugee Coordinator (Location: Manila, Philippines) selected refugee training participants; reviewed and commented on proposed annual budget: monitored ICMC's field operation to [ensure] compliance with all terms and conditions of this agreement with the assistance of a field consultant assigned to this program; assisted ICMC as required in securing visas for employees and assisted when necessary in other matters involving host country policies or procedures. Acted as liaison, as required with the government of the Philippines and UNHCR respecting issues arising from the program; and advised the Project Monitor in Washington of dates and numbers of refugees entering and completing training cycles.
3. Office of the Comproller (Location: Washington, D.C.) reviewed and approved annual budget; and interpreted terms and provisions of agreement when clarification was required:

and reviewed and executed formal amendments to agreement as determined to be appropriate and necessary.

4. Regional Coordinator (Location: Bangkok, Thailand) assisted the Department by providing guidance to ICMC in carrying out the authority and activities set forth; cooperated in the administration of such programs of student testing and data collection as designed for the purpose of assessing student progress as designated by the Bureau's Project Monitor.
5. Refugee Service Center, Center for Applied Linguistics (Location: Manila, Philippines) cooperated with the Center for Applied Linguistics (CAL) to produce Passage, a journal providing an exchange of ESL/CO educational information among the implementing agencies in Southeast Asia and elsewhere, between those field implementors and service providers in the U.S. who teach or otherwise assist refugees. ICMC through designated site editors, was responsible for submitting articles from Bataan to the CAL/Manila editor according to a schedule determined by CAL.
6. ICMC Sub-office (Location: Washington, D.C.) given the significant number of contracts administered by ICMC in the context of the U.S. refugee resettlement program, the ICMC Council in 1984 approved the establishment of a sub-office of the commission in Washington, D.C. to carry out liaison functions with the U.S. Department of State and to handle the hiring of necessary program personnel overseas. Aided for many years in this effort by its American affiliate, the Migration and Refugee Services office of the U.S. Catholic Conference, the Commission nevertheless felt that with the growth of the ESL/CO program in the Philippines and the continued functioning of its seven JVA operations, direct presentation of ICMC with U.S., authorities in Washington had become essential. In addition to its liaison functions with the State Department, the sub-office was also expected to act as a go-between with donor sources among U.S. corporate community (ICMC, 1984b).
7. ICMC General Secretariat (Location: Geneva, Switzerland) coordinated the activities of ICMC affiliates worldwide, providing resettlement opportunities for refugees and migrants. As a contractual partner in the channeling of funds to specific

refugee projects, the office works in close cooperation with governmental and intergovernmental organizations such as the United Nations High Commissioner for Refugees and the Intergovernmental Committee for Migration. Likewise, the General Secretariat serves as a link between refugee assistance affiliates in developing or first asylum countries and donor agencies in Europe and abroad; and also carries out the directives and policies of the ICMC Council and Governing Committee (ICMC, 1984b).

Of the agencies that provided the most on-going to the least cooperation to ICMC/Philippines in the field were conceivably in this order: (1) Refugee Service Center / Center for Applied Linguistics:[28] (2) Department of State, Regional Consultant; (3) Bureau for Refugee Programs, Officer of Training; (4) Refugee Coordinator; (5) ICMC/Sub-Office, Washington, D.C.; (6) Bureau for Refugee Programs, Office of the Comproller; and (7) General Secretariat, ICMC/Geneva.

By posing the question: "What were the agencies that ICMC/ Philippines had regular (written) reporting responsibilities to?" provides insight into how effectively or otherwise guidance functions of the agreement were carried out. Once a month ICMC sent monthly reports of its operational activities to: the Secretary General ICMC/ Geneva: the ESL/CO Regional Consultant; Office of Training; Refugee Coordinator: The Consortium/Thailand; and the Philippine Refugee Processing Center.

The Regional Coordinator, in the course of a year, might travel from Bangkok to PRPC as much as five times and had been known to stay as long as two weeks at a time. In the instance of the Refugee Coordinator where his duties were clearly spelled out and suggested that this office was considered to be the more important as far as having "operational" control of the cooperative agreement in the Philippines, the ICMC monthly report(s), however, showed that for over a period of twenty-four (24) months, the Coordinator and his Field consultant had visited the campsite on an irregular basis.

---

28 The Director of Training, Bureau for Refugee Programs while on her visit to PRPC, announced the planned "phase-down then phase-out" of the CAL regional office in Manila (ICMC, 1988d).

It was generally known that the Refugee Coordinator's primary function was to coordinate the refugee flow into the PRPC as well as the U.S. A plausible argument could be made that this activity was best conducted in Manila where a "reliable" telephone was required to carry out this task, the reason for his scarce presence in the camp.

The Regional Consultant based in Thailand, who made regular visits to the PRPC was the real "linkage" to the cooperative agreement. This operational style of management at the international level can best be termed project management by absentia.

REFERENCES

Amerasia Journal, 1989 By M. Pulido

Baker, et. Al, 1983; Lin and Minoru, 1983

Refugee Service Center, 1986, Rumbaut, 1985

Intercultural Education For Multicultural Societies Albert and Triands, 1985; Cory, 1986; HOfsted, 1986; McCaffery, 1986 Stein, 1981; Tollefson, 1986.

Refugee Education: Friere, 1968; Hughes – Wiener, 1986; Hunter, 1982; RMC, 1984; Starr and Roberts, 1981.

Practical Concepts of Cultural Orientation for Instructional Implementation from 1990 to 1995; Ranard and Pfleger, 1995.

Multi – Ethnic Western Milieu; Cory 1986; Forbes, 1985

Refugee Educational Theory of Refugee Education: Blassingame, 1984; Blume, 1987; Gochenour and Janeway, 1977; Hughes – Wiener, 1986; Tollefson, 1986; Walsh, 1985.

Refugee Resettlement: Brimelow, 1995; Harmon, 1995; Morgan 1995.

The Effects of Pre – entry training on The Resettlement of Indo – Chinese: Final Report RMC, 1984.

ICMC Instructional Program Components: Preparation for American School System (PASS); Work Orientation (WO); English as a Second

Language (ESL), and Cultural Orientation (CO); Program Focus McCafferty, 1986; Redding, 1985; Staff Development Albert 1985; Blassingame, 1984; Blume, 1987; Maciel, 1985; Wederspahn, 1985; Wyly, 1986; Tollefson – Educational Theory 1986, 1989.

U.S. Refugee Resettlement Publications: Information Update RSC/ CAL, 1986 – 87; The Bride IRAC, 1987; The Front Page RSC / CAL, 1987

Theory of Mastery Teaching: Madeline Hunter 1982

Responsible Reduction in Force: An American Management Association Research Report on Downsizing and Outplacement, copyright 1987, New York: American Management Association.

Tollefson Article: Functional Competencies in the U.S. Refugee Program: Theoretical and Practical Problems 1986: TESOL Quarterly

Educational Theory and Pedagogical Development: U.S. Department of State: Chan, 1980; Morgan, 1985; RMC, 1984

Refugee Multi – Cultural Education: Blassingame, 1987; Harrison, 1987; Interaction, 1991

American Dominant Cultural Group: Hall, 1981; Kochman, 1981, Brimelow, 1995; Fujiyoshi, 1989

Minority-of-color Groups: Carter, 1990; Gross, 1991; Ronk, 1991; Wilson, 1987; White, 1988

Refugee Publications of The Center for Applied Linguistics: The Journal, 1981 to 1983; Passage: A Journal of Refugee Education 1985 to 1988; Information Update 1985 to 9188; In America: Perspective on Refugee Resettlement 1988 to 1991

Refugee Day-to-Day Life in the first Asylum Camp: IRAC, 1988; Refugees, 1989

Safe Zone for Refugees: Ngo and Warner, 1987; Robinson, 1987; Richburg, 1989

Basic Educational and Cultural Needs of Refugees: Blassingame, 1984 to 1987; Maciel, 1985; Mydans, 1988; Martin, 1986; Redding, 1985; Thang, 1987; Verzosa, 1988; White, 1988

Philippine Refugee Processing Center: Burns, 1991; Lee 1989; 1988

Refugee Articles: Chicago Tribune; Christian Science Monitor; International Herald Tribune; Life; Manila Bulletin, Newsweek; New York Times; Philippine Star; Refugee Magazines, San Francisco Chronicle; U.S. News and World Report; US Today 1981 to 1988

Refugee life in a Multi – Ethnic Society in America: International Catholic Migration Commission (ICMC) 1984; Morgan, 1995

Filipino Political Affairs Solidarity Conference: 1987; Zich 1986

International Catholic Migration Commission (ICMC) Learning Resource Center (LRC). Philippine Refugee Processing Center (PRPC) Sabang, Morong, Bata-an, Philippines

International Catholic Migration Commission (ICMC) Preparation For American Secondary School (PASS) Program, English as a Second Language (ESL) Language Laboratory, Philippine Refugee Procssing Center (PRPC) Sabang, Morong, Bata-an, Philippines

Printed in the United States
By Bookmasters